Challenges Of Cultural And Racial Diversity To Counseling:

Volume 1

Great Britain And The United States

London Conference Proceedings

Edited by:

Edwin L. Herr, EdD

John McFadden, PhD

Foreword by *Robert J. Nejedlo, PhD*
President, 1988–1989
American Association for Counseling and Development

American Association for Counseling and Development

A Note From the Publisher

This is a selected proceedings of the first international conference sponsored by AACD. Not all of the presenters are represented in this publication. Those papers included were intended as working drafts, and should be considered as such.

Printed in the United States of America

Cover design by Sarah Jane Valdez

CONTENTS

Foreword

At this time in the development of our global society, changes are occurring more rapidly than at any other time in the development of all societies in the history of human civilization. Indeed, who would ever have predicted that the Berlin Wall would come down in November 1989! We are fast becoming a global society, and indeed economic, social, ecological, and political signs demonstrate that no longer can any society afford to exist without interdependence.

As the concept of a global society becomes a reality, it is important that the counseling and human development profession be futuristic in its direction and help its members acquire the awareness and the skills necessary to cope with the changes affecting them as citizens of this global society. It is for this reason that the Anglo/American conference was planned.

During 1988–89, the theme for the American Association for Counseling and Development (AACD) was, "Transformation of the Profession: From Lanterns to Lasers and Beyond." This futuristic theme conveys a sense of redirecting activities with greater precision and specified focus. The five major efforts for the year were: (1) to advance professionals' capabilities as agents of change and developers of potential; (2) to raise members' image and visibility as professionals; (3) to present well-conceived, well-balanced, proactive plans addressing critical issues facing the profession; (4) to highlight and improve association services to members; and (5) to pursue collaborative interpersonal, interdisciplinary, and international efforts. It is readily apparent that an international conference addressing individual and societal needs fulfills a part of each of the above five major efforts.

Another compelling reason for international conferences is that our association's statement of values supports activities that enable positive change by working with other organizations and societies. In July 1988 the American Association for Counseling and Development adopted a set of common values that provide a philosophical and moral base for the existence and work of the association. These values are caring for self and others, enabling positive change, acquiring and using knowledge, empowering leadership, and promoting linkage. It is especially the final value that most vividly provides a raison d'être for international conferences and activities. Specifically, it states, "We believe in fostering an integrative quality, interdependence, and connectedness among people, organizations, and societies." It is a value that indicates our desire to foster positive working relationships among individuals and organizations interpersonally, interprofessionally, and internationally. It is in this spirit of working together internationally to improve the quality of life for peoples in all nations, and with the recognition of our need for interdependence, that the leadership in AACD collaborated with the leadership in the British Association for Counselling (BAC) in planning and implementing our first offshore conference in the history of AACD.

The actual impetus for this conference came following a meeting of approximately 20 national and international leaders during the 1988 AACD convention in Chicago. The importance of working together with other professionals on an international level was highlighted. Following that meeting, a planning committee of AACD leaders was identified. These individuals were: Patrick Christoff, director of professional development; Ajit Das, chair, International Relations Committee; Sunny Hansen, AACD President-elect; Ed Herr, conference co-coordinator; Courtland Lee, president, Association for Multicultural Counseling and Development; P.J. McDonough, executive director of AACD; John McFadden, conference co-coordinator; Nancy Pinson-Millburn, AACD assistant executive director for association and professional relations; Lee Richmond, president, National Career Development Association; Clemmie Solomon, chair, Human Rights Committee; Barbara Brown Robinson, director of association relations; and Bob Nejedlo, president of AACD and chair of the Conference Planning Committee. This group decided to make AACD's first international conference largely a bilateral conference. It was decided that we would focus on relationships between counseling and human development professionals in Britain and the United States. We then sought the participation of leaders in the British Association for Counselling (BAC), and they agreed to cooperate. Working together from Britain were: Judith Baron, BAC chairperson; Derek Hope, conference co-coordinator; Colin Lago, Sheffield University; and Joyce Thompson, British Health Service.

The purpose of the conference was to bring together counselors, including counseling theorists and researchers, and other human development specialists from Britain, the United States, and other countries in the world to examine economic, social, ecological, and political issues related to the roles of counseling and human development in multicultural societies. The theme of the conference was "Challenges of Cultural and Racial Diversity to Counseling in Britain and the United States." The location of the conference was the campus of Brunel University of West London, and the dates were June 25–29, 1989.

Uppermost in the conceptualization and planning for this first international conference was the idea that in any bilateral or international effort, the aim would be to gain awareness of each others' culture and to share ideas of what has seemed to work in one's own culture. It is important that one culture not attempt to implant successful ideas on another culture. Rather, after awareness and sharing, professionals from each culture can put forth the best corroborative thinking and decide for themselves a practical best course of action to address the challenges and issues of their own culture.

It was with this philosophy that the planners of this conference agreed on the format, which consisted of major international plenary speakers representing gender, racial, ethnic, and physical differences. Each of the major speakers addressed one of four areas of challenge to cultural and racial diversity (i.e., economic, social, ecological, and political). Following each plenary session, the participants met in groups of 10–15 to discuss their reactions to issues that the speaker had stimulated. Each discussion group had an appointed group leader and recorder and was asked to make recommendations that later could be carried out by the participants and the sponsoring organizations.

In addition, conference participants were invited to present papers or workshops to address the role of the counselor or human development professional in relation to the economic, social, ecological, or political challenges to cultural and racial diversity. Each afternoon of the conference was devoted to a discussion of the papers and material presented in workshops.

On the final morning of the conference, Edwin Herr and John McFadden summarized the recommendations that resulted from the small group discussions. These recommendations and the edited speeches and papers from the conference are presented in this publication.

Throughout the planning for this conference strong cooperation between the conference leadership from AACD and BAC was evident. Courtland Lee made two trips (on frequent flyer miles) to London and met with the BAC leadership. His liaison work proved invaluable to the success of the conference. Derek Hope did outstanding work in ensuring that the conference facilities were arranged and that the necessary communication among our British colleagues took place. Letters, telephone calls, and the electronic fax were all used as vehicles of communication among the Conference Planning Committee. The planning for this conference was exciting because it was the first such offshore conference, and members of the planning committee worked with great interest and zeal.

All of the planning committee members deserve special thanks and appreciation for competent performance. Their names have been mentioned previously. It was a pleasure to chair this committee and work in the company of astute colleagues in Britain and the United States. In terms of the preparation of this monograph, appreciation is expressed to Rob Hooper of the British Association of Counselling for his editing assistance with some of the presenters' papers. Nancy Pinson-Millburn deserves many thanks for her keen interest, her continuous tracking of information related to the conference, and the procurement of plenary session speakers. We are only sorry she was not able to attend in person. To Ed Herr and John McFadden go my sincere appreciation and heartfelt thanks for working so diligently on the events related to the conference as well as the writing and editing involved in this publication. They worked extremely well together and brought to the conference participants, and now to the readers, a blending of unsurpassed knowledge and experience related to cultural and racial diversity. To them I owe a debt of deep gratitude.

And now, readers, allow me to set the stage for a stimulating, inspirational recollection of the conference proceedings. We are gathered in Lecture Theatre E in the Central Lecture Building on the campus of Brunel University of West London. There are 180 participants of which approximately 50 are from Britain, 10 from European and Asian countries, and 120 from the United States. Ms. Judith Baron, the chairperson of the British Association for Counselling is the first to welcome us to Britain and to the conference. In her kind, courteous, and friendly manner she expresses her pleasure that this Anglo-American conference is taking place. She stresses the importance of examining the critical issues that we as professionals face as we guide and counsel others in making career choices, leading satisfying lives, and coping with societal stressors. Next, I, Bob Nejedlo, as AACD president, extend greetings to those assembled on behalf of the 56,000 members of the American Association for Counseling and Development. I convey the sense of excitement as we are about to begin this historic first international conference and issue the challenge inherent in the conference theme, "Challenges of Cultural and Racial Diversity to Counseling in Britain and the United States." We are inspired with the sense of history of the events that have taken place between Britain and the United States and appreciate what others have done to advance our societies. Especially when we realize that our professional mission is to enhance human development throughout the life span are we compelled to understand the cultural and racial issues in society in order to advocate for and facilitate changes. We receive a final welcome from Dr. P.J. McDonough, AACD executive director, who relays greetings from the central staff at AACD headquarters in Alexandria, Virginia. Dr. McDonough expresses his appreciation to all individuals who have worked to make this conference a reality, and closes with wishes for a successful, productive conference.

You are invited now to read this digest of the conference. Perhaps you, too, will be stimulated by what you read, and further, be challenged to do what *you* can to provide enriched opportunities for people of all cultures.

—Robert J. Nejedlo, PhD, NCC
Chair, Conference Planning Committee
AACD President, 1988–89

PREFACE

Ethnic, racial, and cultural diversity have become prominent concerns of governments, educators, and employers throughout the world. The needs to respect and, indeed, celebrate such diversity have arisen as major political, social, or economic issues in many nations that historically have masked their cultural pluralism by oppression, segregation, discrimination, and other forms of formal or implicit apartheid.

As the quest for freedom and democracy sweeps Eastern Europe, the Soviet Republics, Central America, and Southern Africa, among other geographical regions of the world, at its core is individuals' desire to have their ethnic, racial, or cultural identity valued and protected. They do not want their histories, traditions, and belief systems homogenized by a majority political or economic system. Rather, they want these aspects of themselves and their cultural distinctiveness to be considered and responded to by social institutions and social mechanisms that are sensitive to the implications of cultural differences.

Both Great Britain and the United States have become, as have virtually all the nations of the world, places of transition or transformation. The pressures and strains of international economic competition, shifting family structures, educational reform, growing pluralism among native and immigrant populations, as well as among persons of majority and minority cultures, have added new challenges to the roles of counseling and human development professionals in multicultural societies. Britain and the United States have become microcosms of how these challenges interact in a crucible of cultural pluralism. But such challenges also provide the stimuli for new promise and new paradigms of action for counselors and related professionals.

The mission of the conference at Brunel University in June 1989, from which the substance of this monograph evolved, was to bring together members of the British Association for Counselling and the American Association for Counseling and Development to examine the economic, social, ecological, and political issues related to the roles of counseling and human development in these two multicultural societies. In addition, Anglo-American perspectives focused on how counselors and human development specialists could contribute to the achievement and maintenance of peace as defined in international, regional, or local terms. Integral to such analyses was examining the roles of counselors and other helping professionals as agents of conflict resolution and mediation among culturally different populations, as mentors and guides for persons who seek purpose and self-definition in multicultural environments, and as facilitators of opportunities and brokers of information in societies seeking access and equity for all their members.

In the broadest terms, the challenges of cultural and racial diversity to counseling in Britain and the United States can be highlighted against the background of four interdependent emphases. Each, however, is an area of influence and substance in understanding the possible places of needed intervention by counselors and human development professionals. The four areas include issues that can be described as ecological, economic, social, or political in their essence. These four emphases represent the major content portions of the conference and of this monograph, and thus provide the recommendations for theory, training, policy, and practices presented at the end of this monograph. It is the hope of the conference organizers that these recommendations will be seen as a template for action by governmental and professional organizations as well as by counselors and human development professionals. To this end we the editors and the authors dedicate this monograph. We hope it will be useful as a substantive contribution to the professional literature in cross-cultural counseling and human development. But we also hope that the monograph will spur plans of action to sensitize the "ecologies" of importance to the provision of individual freedom, mobility, and purpose within a world context of cultural pluralism.

—Edwin L. Herr
Pennsylvania State University;

—John A. McFadden
University of South Carolina

The Language of Counseling in the United States and Britain: An Overview[1]

However similar in their shared values for human rights, social equity, and cross-cultural sensitivity, counselors in Britain and the United States differ in how they use the language of counseling and human development. Because counseling is a profession in which words, ideas, and communication are extraordinarily important, we begin our study of the challenges of cultural and racial diversity in Britain and the United States with three brief analyses of the language of counseling in these two nations.

First, from a British perspective is the view of Colin Lago, a counselor at the Student Counseling Service, Sheffield University, England. Second is a summary by Joyce Thompson, a Registered Mental Nurse and Community Psychiatric Nurse with the British Health Service.

Third, from a U.S. perspective is the work of Dr. Courtland E. Lee, associate professor and head of the Counselor Education Program, University of Virginia. Dr. Lee is a past president of the Association for Multi-Cultural Counseling and Editor of the *Journal of Multi-Cultural Counseling.*

Of particular importance to these analyses of British and American counseling is the reality that counseling language and practice are shaped by history and by particular theoretical influences that have not always been inclusive of concerns about cultural diversity or the importance of preparing or nurturing minority persons as counselors. Each of these presentations intertwines some of the cultural history of these nations, with the particular forms of language, definition, and content that have shaped counseling and human development in that country.

---

[1] The attempt has been made to be authentic with regard to language differences and spelling differences, as used by British and American authors/speakers in this Introduction. This would include British terms, such as counselling and centre, which have retained their British spellings. Beyond the introductory articles, we have been consistent with the American spelling purely for production reasons.

The Status of Multicultural Counselling in Britain

Colin Lago

We thought it would be briefly useful to offer you an opportunity of understanding some of the dominant theories of influence in terms of counselling theory in Britain. Obviously person-centered approaches to counselling (e.g., Rogers) have an enormous influence on British counselling practice. So have psychodynamic approaches—the work of Freud, Jung, and Melanie Klein—and Gestalt, transactional analysis, rational emotive, and personal construct theory. These tend to be the primary theories for counsellor training in Britain.

On relating theories to the arena of cross-cultural counselling, if I can call it that, certainly in Britain there is very little research, there are very few publications, but there are many workshops run on the subject. And so for some years now, I certainly—and many other people—have been relying an awful lot on American research, literature, and publications. Thus, a lot of our theoretic influences are American, although we are trying to move toward establishing a British base of practice and comprehending its meaning.

Having trained as a counsellor, I went to work in a Midland city called Leicester in about 1978 and soon heard that there was going to be an annual conference of the British Association for Counselling (BAC) and its title was "Counselling Minorities." That title included sexual minorities, political minorities, and so on. My colleague at that time and myself were invited to help organize several workshops at this annual conference. Out of that came the development of an interactive video approach that I shall be using in my workshops tomorrow. Also out of that conference came an ongoing professional group that was multicultural, multiracial, and multiprofessional. We met monthly over about 18 months and tried out different training methods on each other, and in doing so we began to sow an awful lot of seeds of later developments.

As a result of some of these initiatives, in 1980, my colleague and I put up some propositions to the British Association for Counselling. I think they are useful in laying a basis for the British end of things here. We put up four resolutions—the first was that the association accepts the need for greater awareness and concern on the part of its members of the importance of exploring the nature of counselling in a multiracial society. The second resolution was that the association should press for counselling training courses to include course elements that will serve to increase an awareness of (a) the situations of different ethnic groups, including the experience of racism in the United Kingdom, (b) the complexity of counselling clients from a different cultural background, (c) an awareness of the counsellor's own prejudices, sympathies, and predispositions, and (d) the need to debate about whether counselling can or even should occur between White counsellors and Black clients. At that point, BAC had very few Black counsellors. The third and fourth proposals were that the British Association for Counselling should aim to attract more members from the various minority communities living in the United Kingdom, and the the association should offer opportunities for ongoing debate concerning the suitability or not of the notions of counselling for the various minority groups. As a consequence, BAC established the Race Subcommittee.

In 1982, after we had had a year to work on this new committee, we put up two other resolutions. This was the preamble: Two years ago the British Association for Counselling unanimously adopted four resolutions in relation to counselling within a multiracial society. These hinted at but did not specify the extent to which racist practices can be self-perpetuating, invisible to the propagators, in our case counsellors and the institutions within which we work, and can result in harmful consequences for clients and counsellors. Racism damages both those who impose it and those who suffer it. Racism is the implementation of racially prejudiced attitudes, however subtle, by using political, economic, institutional, or personal power. In the light of the former BAC resolutions—as a result of the continuing dialogue within the working party—we wished to propose the following resolutions; the first was: In the acknowledgment that racism in our society creates widespread distress and tension for individuals, families, and within institutions, it is proposed that BAC undertake the task of seeking to recognize, monitor, confront, and eliminate racism in (a) ourselves, (b) the divisions and structure of BAC, and (c) in our individual work as counsellors or trainers and in our developmental work with institutions.

There were three other resolutions: that the association should publish a statement to this effect both within and outside the organization, and that the association should formally adopt the Racism Awareness in Counselling in Education Working Party. This working party was established at the Counselling and Education Counselling Exchange in 1983 as a development from the work of the 1979 conference. It was by the formal adoption of this Race Subcommittee that we then wanted to get the association to monitor training courses in this context. I trained in the late 70s and not a hint was mentioned of issues due to cultural race. And I think that is still the case for many courses in Britain. The final resolution was that the BAC actively seek to attract the expertise of more Black counsellors. I think historically this takes the history of BAC up to about 1983 or 1984.

Multicultural Counselling in Britain: Perspectives on Race and Cultural Education

Joyce Thompson

I will try to bring you up to date with what we are doing in the Race Subcommittee. Colin Lago has told you about the way the group started. I have been chair of that group for the last 2 years, and one of our major tasks is to continue to ensure that we don't collude with diluting issues on racism, issues that deal with race and culture. A lot of education in Britain today tends to dilute multicultural issues when actually dealing with issues of race, and in doing that, the power issue does not get addressed, so we therefore hide behind talking about culture when we are talking about issues of race and neglect to address the influences that the power structure in this country has and is playing in those issues. Therefore, the Race Subcommittee is about to change its name. We no longer wish to be called the Race Awareness Counselling in Education Group. We wish to be called the Race and Cultural Education Group of a Counselling Section of BAC to reflect more accurately what we are doing. We are looking at issues of race and culture in a broader context than in the educational context where we started.

One of the things that has happened since the formation of the Race Group is that we have gone out from that group to look for our brothers and sisters who are involved in counselling because we couldn't find them. We knew there were a lot of Black people out there who were very qualified and experienced counsellors, but we didn't know where they were, and so we decided to look for them and we found them and formed a group called the Association of Black Counsellors, which gives support to Black people—both professionals and nonprofessionals. We also are involved actively in training, and last year we had a first national conference that was a joint conference between ABC—the Association of Black Counsellors—and the Race Group. It was a very successful conference, and there are some conference reports for sale for a pound each if anyone wishes to buy them.

Colin Lago mentioned the theories that were behind counselling in Britain today. The one he didn't actually mention was revaluation core counselling. A lot of Black people seem to be gravitating toward revaluation core counselling. Maybe it is because it addresses the influence and the oppression that people need to get in touch with and work through. I think I need to finish off by saying that both ABC and Race Group are committed to working together. What we want to continue doing is to explore the complex issues that surround the sort of language we use in counselling. The language of counselling in Britain does not necessarily address issues that take into consideration the diversity of the people we are dealing with. And so a lot of Black people, for example, do not go to counsellors because the counselling is a very White, liberal, middle class activity, and the language that is spoken does not reach them. Hence, we felt that it was extremely important in the time we have together in these next few days to pay attention to the sort of language we use in counselling and how we can make sure that this language caters to all sections of the community.

Multicultural Counseling: The American Perspective

Courtland E. Lee

American society has experienced tremendous change over the past two decades. The turmoil of the civil rights movement of the 1960s, for example, gave rise to a recognition that the United States is a pluralistic, rather than a monolithic, society. This recognition has brought forth the initial phase of a period in our national history that may be referred to as the *era of cultural pluralism*. Cultural pluralism, or "unity in diversity," is a goal based on the belief that the dominant culture will benefit from coexistence and interaction with the cultures of groups that have historically held minority status. A basic feature of cultural pluralism is the process of developing a new mainstream culture through the equal cooperation and fusion of separate cultural groups.

Cultural pluralism, as a concept, refutes the archaic notion that American society is a melting pot. Instead, the America of today and tomorrow must be reconceptualized as a *salad bowl,* where each ingredient keeps its distinctive taste and properties, while contributing to the overall character and flavor of the salad.

The concept of cultural pluralism receives its impetus not only from the great economic, legislative, and social gains made by Americans of African descent during the civil rights struggles of the 1960s, but more recently, from the wave of immigration from Southeast Asia, the Caribbean basin, and Central America. This new immigration phenomenon has brought people with new hues and world views to the United States.

Significantly, cultural pluralism is being increasingly reflected in the American educational system and work force. For example, the U.S. Department of Education reports that whereas the population of school age children in America's schools has declined over the last decade, the percentage of students of color has increased from 24% in 1976 to 29% in 1984. The DOE forecasts that by the year 2000, 40% of the youth in the nation's schools will be from ethnic groups of color. Some concrete examples from around the United States help to underscore this projection:

- For example, more than 35% of the children in San Francisco public schools do not speak English, or speak limited English.
- Two thirds of the kindergarten students in Los Angeles are Hispanic (a term used in the United States to describe those people of Spanish, African, and North and South American Indian cultural heritage).
- One in every six elementary school children in Beverly Hills, California, is Iranian.
- A high school in Dearborn, Michigan, has separate physical education classes to respect the segregation of the sexes required under Moslem law in deference to the Arab students in the school.
- At Halsey High School in Queens, New York, students speak 34 languages and dialects including Persian, Hindi, Russian, Portuguese, Cantonese, and Spanish.
- At J.E.B. Stuart High School in Fairfax County, Virginia, there are over 60 languages spoken among the student body.

As for data about the American work force, it has been projected that by the beginning of the 21st century, approximately 75% of those entering the world of work in the United States will be people of color and women.

With data such as these, what are the implications for counseling professionals concerning cultural diversity in America? It is becoming more and more evident to American counseling professionals that a major implication is that present and future counseling must be inclusive: It can no longer concern itself solely with one class of client or one cultural/ethnic group. In addition, although a great deal of the knowledge base for counseling across cultures grew out of the African-American struggle for equality, we in America have come to realize that multicultural counseling can no longer be considered only as "counseling Black people effectively."

Given these implications, let me turn to an often perplexing question that faces American counseling professionals attempting to deliver services in an increasingly diverse society: *What is multicultural or cross-cultural counseling?* Over the last decade, many terms have sprung up in the American mental health field that reflect the notion of culture in counseling. Among these are: *transcultural counseling, cross-cultural counseling,* and *counseling the culturally different.* Although all of these terms have a common focus, subtle differences in their meanings have created much confusion among American counseling professionals. Some of this confusion was alleviated in the spring of 1986, when the Association of Multicultural Counseling and Development (AMCD) held its first national symposium in Atlanta, Georgia. This symposium brought together some of the leading American theorists and practitioners in the field of counseling and cultural pluralism (some of whom are here at this conference). One of the goals of the symposium was to formulate an operational term to define the theory and practice of counseling across cultures in American society. The consensus of symposium participants was that the term "multicultural counseling" reflected the spirit and intent of counseling in a culturally pluralistic society.

What, then, is *multicultural counseling* in an American context? Simply defined, it is a relationship between a counselor and a client that takes both the personal *and* cultural experiences of the counselor *and* the client into consideration in the helping process.

Whenever culture is considered as a variable in counseling, it can become a source of conflict and misunderstanding, leading to barriers between counselors and clients who differ in terms of cultural background. Within American society, it must be understood that in traditional terms counseling is an activity that represents *White, European, European-American middle class male-dominated* culture. The counseling profession in general, therefore, holds certain generic values and characteristics that are frequently different from those of ethnic groups of color in American society, which often represent world views whose origins are Africa, Asia, South America, and other areas of the Third World. Recently, the Council for Accreditation of Counseling and Related Educational Programs (CACREP, the accrediting body that assures quality in American counselor training programs) approved a set of multicultural skills competencies developed by AMCD as *guidelines* for counselor educational programs in the preparation of multicultural counselors. It is anticipated that those programs that adopt these guidelines in the course of seeking accreditation will expose their students to counseling theory and practice that represent culturally diverse points of view regarding mental health and human development. The hope of many counselor educators in the United States is that with these guidelines they will be able to train a generation of counseling professionals who have the awareness, knowledge, and skills to intervene effectively in the lives of culturally diverse clients.

I hope this gives you a brief overview of multicultural counseling in the United States. Now let's spend the next few days exploring our differences and commonalities as counseling professionals representing different, but similar, countries and cultural dynamics. Let's engage in shared activities, that in the spirit of Anglo-American cooperation, will help us to address the challenges of cultural diversity to counseling in both our societies collectively, both now and in the future.

PART I

ECOLOGICAL ISSUES

Neither counselors nor the problems that clients bring to counselors exist in a cultural vacuum. Nor do the "psychologies" that explain individual human behavior occur independently of the psychosocial contexts in which they were formulated. Behavior tends to occur in relation to a context, in transaction with an environment that is composed of metaphors, reinforcements, and events to which individual behavior is typically a reaction. In such transactions, the fit between models of behavior valued by majority cultures and those of minority cultures frequently come into conflict, create problems in communication and understanding, and trigger anxiety, confusion, conflict, interpersonal dysfunctions, or other individual and social turmoil. In a fundamental sense, problems of individual "fit" in a cultural, physical, or social context constitute ecological issues. It is this theme that occupies the authors of the papers included in part 1.

The first plenary paper was presented by Edwin L. Herr and addressed "Ecological Challenges to Counseling in a World of Cultural and Racial Diversity." John A. McFadden reacted to this paper and extended it in its application to Black populations, as did Sara E. Melendez to Hispanic populations. Edwin L. Herr is distinguished professor of education and head, Department of Counselor Education, Counseling Psychology and Rehabilitation Services Education, The Pennsylvania State University; John A. McFadden is the Benjamin E. Mays Professor of Education at the University of South Carolina; Sara E. Melendez is vice provost of the University of Bridgeport.

Following the plenary papers, part 1 concludes with two papers presented in the conference's discussion/workshop groups. Both papers apply ecological and cultural insights to the application of counseling. In the first paper, Ian R. Owen, a social therapist in London, identifies and describes anthropological concepts of importance to counseling in his paper, "The Application of Some Ideas From Anthropology to Counseling, Therapy and Cross-Cultural Counseling." In the second paper, C. Scully Stikes, assistant chancellor of student affairs at the University of Wisconsin-Milwaukee, discusses the implications of authentic counseling approaches to international models of counseling in his paper, "An International Model of Counseling: The Authentic Counseling Model."

ECOLOGICAL CHALLENGES TO COUNSELING IN A WORLD OF CULTURAL AND RACIAL DIVERSITY

Edwin L. Herr

At the outset, it is useful to note that it is note overly grandiose to contend that the underlying issues central to this conference are ecological in origin. In broad terms, ecology is the study of the interaction between organisms and their environments (Blocker, 1987). The other three themes of the conference—political, economic, and social—are specific manifestations of ecological processes, of individual-environment transactions, in their impact on defining the metaphors as well as the actualities within which human behavior is permitted, encouraged, or free to function. Therefore, through whichever of the ecological "windows" one chooses to look to try to understand human behavior *as it is* or *as it might be,* one finds the effects of the interface of the physical, social, political, economic, and psychological environments individuals occupy and the behavioral responses they produce in relation to such interfaces or transactions. One also finds that such ecological contexts are not standardized within or across nations. The environments individuals experience in a society are likely to differ depending upon whether one is a member of the majority or minority culture, the in-group or the out-group, a native born resident or immigrant, a man or woman, a person of color or White, a person of a particular religious tradition or none at all.

Ecological Issues Defined

When ecological issues for counseling are considered, it is not unusual to emphasize the first definition that traditionally appears in a dictionary. To wit, Ecology is "1. The branch of biology that deals with the relations between living organisms and their environment" (Webster, 1983). When that definition is the focus of concern, the discussion tends to center on the worldwide threats to the survival of living beings on this planet. These include: changing weather patterns; the "greenhouse effect" with its predicted outcomes of warming global temperatures and causing crop failures and health problems; industrial pollution and smog, with their threat to drinking water or to the air being breathed; unbridled population growth in some parts of the world and the accompanying fears about wide-ranging malnutrition, limited economic opportunity, and infanticide; terrorism as a physical threat to life among the innocent and as a psychological threat to free movement around the world; the AIDS epidemic as reflective of the inability of immune systems to combat certain types of viruses that may lie dormant for a long period of time and then flare up in various populations, particularly those under intense stress; drug and alcohol abuse, the products of ingested physical substances that are addictive and enslaving. These ecological issues are not isolated to a small part of the earth's governments or populations. Nor are they only physical or biological in their manifestations. They spawn anxiety, information deficits or distortions, fear, stress-related diseases, posttraumatic stress syndromes, and other emotional and psychological concerns that become the content of counseling and guidance services.

But, as important as the physical ecology is for the survival of the human species, it is equally necessary to consider a second definition of ecology: "2. In sociology, the relationship between the distribution of human groups with reference to material resources and the consequent social and cultural patterns" (Webster, 1983). That definition of ecology indicates that persons of different racial or cultural backgrounds are likely to experience habitats, life spaces, environments, resource availability, and ecological contexts that are in fact different because of their cultural or racial characteristics. Therefore, ecological impacts on human behavior are likely to vary in degree and probably in kind depending upon one's status in a given society. In essence, ecological approaches affirm that human behavior does not occur in a vacuum. It occurs in a complex manner in response to environmental stimuli, social metaphors, traditions, and meaning or value structures that define the psychological and physical boundaries within which various populations function in their daily behavioral transactions.

Ecological issues are not unidimensional. The interactions among the various aspects of one's life space exert influences or limits on how gender and family roles are conceived, the achievement images likely to be nurtured, the resources available, and the accuracy and forms of knowledge provided about opportunities. In these respects, societies can be likened to percolators of information and reinforcement, the flow and substance of which is filtered by cultural, socioeconomic, and racial factors. For example, a poor person is not simply a rich person without money. A poor person by definition has experienced a different ecology and ecologies than has a rich person. The poor person's information, reinforcements, and resources are likely to be significantly different from those available to a rich person. So is the poor person's likely belief system or sense of self-efficacy about personal power to gain an education or the skills necessary to improve his or her lot in life or to increase life chances. Thus, a person's ecology affects his or her philosophy of life, sense of self-worth, and power to change life circumstances or to alter ecological contexts.

Cultural and racial diversity are not unrelated to matters of economics and life chances. For example, persons of color in a predominantly White culture are likely to be poorer, less well educated on the average, and have less access to material resources and fewer savings and other support systems that allow planning and acting upon long-term goals. They are more likely to attribute an external locus of control to their life course than an internal locus of control. They are more likely to live where industrial pollution, poor sanitation, chronic physical ailments, stress, victimization, and alcohol and drug abuse are more the norm than is true for members of affluent or majority cultures. Therefore, the psychology of choice and identity and the interaction of physical, economic, and social or cultural ecologies is different for persons at different socioeconomic levels in any society. Because of the strong correlations between socioeconomic status and gender or race or culture in virtually all societies, the ecology of growth, personal security, and educational and occupational opportunity vary dramatically for persons differentially described by these characteristics.

Limited Counseling Models Amidst Behavioral Diversity

Given such premises it is important to observe that in pluralistic societies, like Great Britain and the United States—where cultural and racial diversity are the norm, not the exception—the assumptions and techniques of counseling have frequently ignored such cultural or racial differences or treated them as benign (Clark, 1987). Counseling models have primarily addressed *intra*cultural phenomena, not *inter*cultural phenomena. Counseling theories and practice have tended to take a universalistic view (Sue, 1978) of human behavior rather than fully acknowledging the cultural distinctiveness in information processing, worldviews, cognitive mechanisms, individual or group reference points for behavior, representations of normality, or behavioral expectations that vary among different groups and many individuals in any society.

There is a danger in applying theories and techniques within the limits of a specific culture to persons of different cultural backgrounds: If one does not acknowledge cultural differences among people that are explanatory of normal variations in behavior across groups, it becomes easy to resort to one approved model of behavior. That model may, in turn, assume the role of the target to be reinforced in counseling. Any behavioral deviation from the approved model is then associated with a "deficit model." The latter suggests that perspectives or activities different from those in the intracultural, universalistic, majority or target model are inferior or abnormal. The next step often is to assume that the deficit, abnormality, or inferiority (as classified in a deficit model) is within the individual rather than within the ecology experienced or the model of normal or appropriate behavior used. Therefore, individuals who may be acting quite consistently with the survival skills required by their environment or with their cultural traditions may be inaccurately characterized as behaviorally aberrant through an *intra*cultural model different from their own.

For cultural or racial subpopulations in a majority or adopted culture, distinctive cultural, ethnic, or racial traditions and their original roots in other nations or social structures persist for long periods of time in self-concepts and behavioral norms. These factors shape behavior and form the base of the interactions that compose a counseling relationship whether it occurs one on one, in a group setting, or within a family therapy context.

Multiple Ecologies Exist

In our second definition of ecology as a sociological perspective, there is a convergence of social history, culture, and racial differences as factors associated with ecological differences. From a broad perspective, there is not one physical ecology nor one social, economic, or political ecology. There are multiple ecologies with which individuals and groups have interacted and do interact, and in the process distinctive cultures have been created that both interpret the ecologies at issue and provide guides to behavior within these ecologies. In this sense cultures are similar to maps or templates about ecological conditions. These maps help persons organize their reality, provide behavioral sanctions, create perceptual cues about matters to which they should attend and give meaning, and define appropriate self-perceptions and manners of expression.

Cultures—as expressions of social, economic, and political ecologies—attribute meaning to psychological and physical events, and in so doing reduce ambiguity and increase predictability for their members. Cultural attributions of meaning provide structures or classification systems by which to sort out and interpret the constant profusion of signals or messages from the environment that every individual experiences daily. Culturally mediated interpretations and predispositions ultimately end up in the cognitions of the individual as assumptions and symbolic representations of a world that is in the last analysis unique to each individual, and in a less specific sense, unique to different cultural groups.

Extending such views, for example, to those of selected family therapists (e.g. Spiegel, 1982), ecological approaches to ethnic families can be seen as synonymous with transactional field approaches; approaches that give major emphases not so much to internal family dynamics as to the family's interaction with external systems and institutional contexts. On the negative side, such an approach looks at the ecological dynamics that have impinged upon the family and caused many of its difficulties; on the positive side, such an approach challenges counselors to help persons to reconnect with networks such as extended families, social support systems, and friends or significant others who can defuse or otherwise alter family dysfunctions. Illustrative of the point, Hines and Boyd-Franklin (1982) contended that in working effectively with Black families in the United States, therapists must be open to exploring "the impact of the social, political, socioeconomic, and broader environmental conditions on the families they treat" (p. 99). Citing the work of Aponte (1979), who used the term *ecostructural* to describe this broader ecological treatment approach and the need to always consider a family's environment and community as relevant to the diagnostic process and planning of treatment, Hines and Boyd-Franklin contended that "the ecostructural reality of poor, inner-city Black families is that the external systems are likely to impinge on them. These may include welfare, the courts, schools, Medicaid, food stamps, and public housing. To treat the family without considering these systems and their impact on family behavior would be a grave error." As Aponte asserted, "we cannot consider the social context as an occasional concern when a family is poor." There are survival issues in such ecological contexts that take precedence over family conflicts. With such families, family therapists must frequently define themselves as system guides who help families learn how to negotiate the complexities of the social service, bureaucratic system more effectively, and to use available resources and contacts to facilitate change.

Whether one talks specifically about family therapy, Black inner-city families, or other counseling issues, in the fullest sense the emphasis of this conference on ecological issues in their various manifestations is a response to the observation of Bronfenbrenner (1979) a decade ago in which he stated: "Human development is properly viewed as a product of the interaction between the developing person and the environment but in practice there is an overwhelming focus on the properties of the person and only the most rudimentary conception and characterization of the environment in which the person is found" (p. 16).

Bronfenbrenner's observations remind us that the dilemmas persons experience and the substance of the problems with which they have to cope do not typically arise without triggering mechanisms external to the person. In large measure, the personal questions for which people seek help are really functions of how they view current social or occupational expectations and opportunities; their feelings of personal significance; whether or not and how much other people depend on them; the availability of free choice, achievement, self-initiative, prestige, role differentiation, and autonomy; and many other matters. The resulting anxieties, information deficits, or indecisiveness these people experience is the content with which counselors and related professionals are concerned. These dilemmas, tasks, and conflicts frequently manifest themselves in mental health problems (e.g., depression) and in interpersonal dysfunctions within the family, the social group, or the workplace. These become both the concerns of counseling and the interactive layers of anxiety and confusion in which such concerns are wrapped and that must be disentangled in the counseling process (Herr, 1989).

Within a complex global environment, one of the growing insights from the ecological issues embracing science and technology is that most of the world's problems today are not really technical or scientific problems, but human problems. As we have altered the physical ecology by fouling pristine waters with oil spills or the atmosphere with fluorocarbons, or decreased the world's oxygen supply by cutting down much of the world's forests, or brought many species to near extinction either by killing them through greed or because we considered them to be nuisances, we have simultaneously caused human problems, particularly for the least advantaged among us. These are the persons whose cultural or racial diversity in a particular nation often makes them most vulnerable to the direct effects on the world's physical ecology that have accompanied scientific and technological implementation. There are those who would remind us that all of us, regardless of cultural and racial diversity, are a product of this life system and are inextricably linked to all parts of it. Our very survival depends on the air, water, and sun and indeed on the allocation of these among humankind. By treating these elements or, indeed, other living beings disrespectfully, we are disrespectful of ourselves (Bellak, Madsen, Sullivan, Swidler, & Tipton, 1985). Such a view raises questions in turn about the status of the world's moral ecologies and the vitality of the institutions that tie the individual to family, community, church, synagogue, mosque, or the nation. It also raises questions about the status of a moral ecology that allows persons to exploit others indiscriminately, injure them psychologically, keep them captive, or kill them.

Moral Ecology

"Since human beings are presently having an enormous impact on the planet earth, (in their unquenchable quest to conquer and exploit it) ecology as a science has close connections to ecology as a philosophy and as a social movement. While ecological science and ecological social philosophy are not identical ... there is no way to keep them separate since every ecological fact has ethical significance" (Bellak et al., 1985, p. 284).

To return to the issue that modern scientific and technological achievements are accompanied by human problems, the point is that in addition to the destructive consequences these processes have often held for the natural ecology, they have frequently had comparable destructive consequences for social ecology. Social ecology is damaged not only by war, genocide, and political repression. It is also damaged by the destruction of the subtle ties that bind human beings to one another, leaving them frightened and alone. Such conditions are compounded by the reality that much of what makes our world and our neighborhoods unsafe arises from economic and racial inequality. Poverty is a crippler of motivation, of dreams, of energy. Without these it is difficult to care about oneself or others. In many places in the world, to be racially or culturally different is also to be poor.

The evidence of ecological effects upon human behavior is wide and sometimes difficult to capture clearly, but illustrative examples can be cited. Selkin (quoted in Robins & Kulbak, 1988) has, for example, demonstrated that suicide mortality varies with social integration, social structure, and social change. High suicide rates have been found with considerable regularity to be associated with unemployment and with economic depression (Platt & Kreitman, 1985; Platt,1984; Wasserman, 1984). In many instances, communities with high unemployment rates also have features that Durkheim and others have defined as "social disorganization"—crime, broken families, secularism. Other data at the family level show that not only is unemployment associated with an increase in the unemployed individual's mental health problems, early death, suicide rates, and stress-related diseases, but also with drug and alcohol abuse, spouse abuse, and child abuse. The effects of unemployment "ripple" through the family and other systems of which people are a part, carrying with it ecological transitions in status and identity that are destructive to personhood and lead to grieving, mourning, and feelings of victimization. The connection to our topic is, of course, in two dimensions: One, unemployment creates dramatic ecological transitions for total family systems that are not only economic but psychological and social as well and, two, frequently those first unemployed or whose employment history is jagged are members of cultural or racial minority groups.

Another subtle but significant ecological issue that is both economic and technical is that associated with advanced technology as a major process of urban-regional restructuring of job availability and population location around the world. The implementation of high or advanced technology brings expectations and requirements that alter the environments in which they are located and the kinds of people who are likely to live in such areas. The location of high-tech manufacturing or information industries is not a random event. Rather, the geography, the demographics, and the political environment of a location have much to do with its suitability for the application of advanced technologies in their many forms. But, the issues for our topic are somewhat different.

Introduction of advanced technology into a community changes its economic and social ecology. Regional differences across a nation increase rather than decrease as high or advanced technologies are introduced into the manufacturing, information, and distribution sectors of a society; people in these regions thus experience major disparities in occupational opportunities, quality of life, education and training, and other areas. These conditions frequently stimulate migration within and across national boundaries, urban congestion and stress, potential widening of gaps between rich and poor, and an erosion of family and community support systems. They also contribute to a dilution of feelings of personal responsibility for one's fate and a blurring of behavioral sanctions that control individual behaviors; changing family structures; and other risk factors that create a seedbed for mental health problems and hold implications for the content of counseling.

Obviously, it is unfair and inaccurate to attribute to the pervasive influence of the implementation of advanced technology across the world all the causal effects on immigration, changing family structures, or being placed "at risk" of psychological, academic, or occupational vulnerability. But, however one talks about these human problems, they are stimulated by ecological change or an ecology—political, economic, moral, social, or physical—for which the "goodness of fit" for certain persons is not adequate. Immigration is certainly a case in point. The Mexican immigrants to the southern United States, the Southeast Asian "boat people," the dissidents from the Eastern block nations, or the persons from many of the British Commonwealth nations or former colonies come to the United States and Britain to find political or economic opportunities that their homes of origin did not afford them. Many come because their ecologies—economic, political, social—do not afford them the opportunity to be competent and integrated citizens, in whatever unique terms that may mean. Before immigration, they typically experienced rejection, a lack of nurturance, ennui, powerlessness, feelings of helplessness, and a desire for better conditions for their children so intense that they risked the pain associated with losing a cultural identity. They risked disrupting their kinship system or extended family system, starting over in occupations beneath their former skill levels and being functionally illiterate in a new language, their fluency in their native language unacknowledged.

The Family as an Ecological Issue

Another ecological issue of major importance is the changing structure and impact of the family. Certainly in America, the nostalgic and traditional view of family is rapidly fading in which mother, father, and two children, in a well-ordered, stable living relationship, where the father is the unquestioned breadwinner and the mother is the homebound nurturant caregiver, is seen as the typical family unit. Such a nuclear family unit, rather than being the majority family pattern, is rapidly becoming the exception, a rarity. In its place, blended families where two previously divorced parents bring the children of prior unions into a new unit or, instead, where as a function of divorce there is only one parent in the home to raise the children, or the nuclear family unit where both parents work, are all becoming common family units of the day. These and other new family configurations that are emerging bring with them new stresses and strains, new definitions of the family as an ecological unit, and new implications for child-rearing and development.

A very important matter in the changing family ecology is the number of families in which both parents work outside the home. Although some women undoubtedly work because they want a career and pursue it in positive terms, many other women work for economic reasons, the need to maintain a standard of living or financial viability in the home. In 1985, in the United States, nearly half of all women with children under age 18 were in the labor force, compared with less than 40% in 1970 (Hayghe, 1986). Only 3 out of 10 women are full-time homemakers. Fundamental to the issue of a changing family ecology is the growing evidence that the norms of childhood are being redefined in many U.S. homes. For example, estimates now place the number of children who come home from school to an empty house in the United States at six million due to the influx of more mothers into the labor force (Turkington, 1983).

These are the so-called "latchkey children" who have received increasing attention because of concern that lack of adult supervision will lead to sexual precocity, vandalism, chemical dependency, and other social problems. By definition, the term "latchkey children" refers to children and youth, unsupervised by their parents, "who care for themselves before or after school, on weekends and during holidays while their parents work" (Robinson, Rowland, & Coleman, 1986). In inner cities where poor single parents and minority families work from necessity, the lack of adult supervision leaves children prone to the influence of "gangs" or cults that become surrogate families and exert concentrated peer pressure to engage in activities that are often antisocial. Such circumstances can result in the lack of integration of young people into their society and to feelings of being uninterested, disconnected, and even hostile to the people and activities in the environment outside of the gang or cult with whom they have identified.

Changes in the family and in the child-rearing environment are, in fact, only one of the forces that conspire to isolate children from the rest of society and parents from support systems that could be of help to them by providing additional adult care-providers in the natural environment of the child. Such forces include the fragmentation of the extended family, the separation of residential and business areas, zoning ordinances, occupational mobility, child-labor laws, the abolition or reduction of the apprentice system, consolidated schools, supermarkets, television, separate patterns of social life for different age groups, the working mother, and the delegation of child care to specialists outside the home. These and other factors have operated to decrease the opportunity and incentive for interaction, affection, identification with, and support between children and older adults. Within this context, the concept of latchkey children may only be the tip of the iceberg, but it is a significant issue.

The example of latchkey children illustrates how the physical and social ecologies of different groups of children vary and how such differences are likely to result in long-term effects on and concerns about child development. It also illustrates how racially and culturally diverse groups who are not part of the majority culture are likely to experience a greater impact from such circumstances than are other more affluent groups with more day-care options. In addition, the latchkey phenomenon illustrates the fact that the economic ecology of a society can also have a major impact on the social and, indeed, the moral ecology of the society. For example, research studies show that one of the constants among working parents is an ambivalence about the arrangements that require their children to go home alone after school and remain alone from approximately 3:00 p.m. until 6:00 p.m. and later. But certainly poorer parents, single parents, or two-earner families who work to maintain economic viability typically feel that they have no choice but to leave the children under self-care because of the expense or lack of availability of child care, and transportation problems. In such instances, social technology in the form of affordable and safe after-school child care has not kept pace with the changing needs for such care because of the demographic shifts in who is entering the workforce, the larger proportion of women with children under 18, and the unevenness of such options for different population groups in the society.

Such circumstances are likely to increase the role of counselors in changing the ecological dimensions in which the latchkey phenomenon is embedded. Indeed, counselors may find themselves working with either latchkey children themselves or with their parents. Or, they may work in behalf of latchkey children. Direct counseling services to latchkey children may involve addressing their feelings of self-confidence and security or their specific fears; it may also involve creating support for these children to help them consider their attitudes about self-care and to share the ways they handle their experiences. For parents, counselors can create opportunities to inform them of the various options and alternatives available to their children; form parent clusters whose schedules might permit rotation of child caregiving; or provide support groups and information for parents to help them deal with their apprehension about leaving their children alone.

Ecological Issues are Multidimensional

The variety of intervention strategies just suggested reflects several further perspectives. One is that most ecological issues are multidimensional: They frequently engender stress and perhaps fear; they alter options available to people; they often require people to have access to new information and to be helped to process it; and, they typically necessitate collective action and the initiation of support mechanisms to provide nurturance, security, and the reduction of feelings of being alone or abandoned in the wake of the particular ecological content.

Space limitations prohibit discussion of many other ecological challenges to counseling in contemporary society. These take many forms: alterations in occupational structures; rising educational and skill level requirements in the work force; the shifting social psychology of work as power, information, and career paths change as a result of the pervasive adaptation of advanced technology; the growing relationships between literacy or its lack and the availability of life options and/or social problems; and the increasing numbers of persons defined as being at risk of becoming physically ill or abused, experiencing mental disorders, or being economically disadvantaged or vulnerable to other forms of negative psychological, social, physical, or economic life events. These are not mutually exclusive factors. Persons who experience unusual amounts of stress from chaotic and disorganized family situations, such as losing a job or being constantly thwarted through prejudice and discrimination in their efforts to become part of the social mainstream, are likely to manifest physical symptoms and stress-related disease, mental disorders, chemical dependency, and possibly abusive or violent behavior. Although it is ultimately an individual who is "at risk," membership in culturally or racially distinctive groups tends to be seen as increasing the likelihood that one will be exposed to the number and severity of factors that lead to behavioral disorders, problematic behavior, or disadvantagement or restricted opportunity. In federal legislation and in policies, theory, or research in the United States, special populations at risk are often described as the physically handicapped, the socially and emotionally disabled, the mentally retarded, the emotionally or educationally disadvantaged, single parents, incarcerated or ex-offenders, dislocated workers, members of specific minority, racial, or ethnic groups, the aging, and the elderly. Within these groups, there are typically subgroups at even greater risk because they are suicidal, functionally illiterate, poverty-stricken, homeless, or otherwise extremely vulnerable to social, economic, or political forces.

In a broad sense, the groups "at risk" identified above are so defined for one of two reasons. According to Perry (1982), the first category comprises all those special populations for whom "historically and at present, cultural stereotypes, the legal system, processes of socialization, and corrosive social stigma operate to provide a negative social-psychological ecology: women, racial and cultural minorities, the elderly, the handicapped, learning-disabled or gifted children, and other groups, such as the mentally ill, the incarcerated, and persons of alternative sexual orientation. The second major category consists of persons who are at significant points of transition and stress in their lives. Thus, these changing 'developmental' special populations are cross-sections of the population at times of...pre- and post-natal care, early childhood support and day care systems...school-employment transitions, illness and death in the family, separation and divorce, career transitions, periods of unemployment and retirement" (p. 52).

To put these observations into our context, the first category of persons at risk are so described because of the ecological effects—political and social—that have classified them in ways that have decreased their mobility and reduced the psychological nurturance available to them; in the second category of persons, the effects are less from a constant bias incorporated into the social and political ecology and more from ecological transitions they have experienced in the family, the workplace, and in their personal status vis-à-vis such transactions. These populations are at risk because at certain developmental or transitional points they have experienced psychological or physical trauma, crises, or other conditions that have caused them to be unusually prone to extraordinary stress, abuse, or other emotional and behavioral disorders. Some persons are at risk because of historical, social, legal, and educational inequities and also because of developmental or transitional problems. In fact, they are in both categories of risk, not one or the other.

As one reviews the literature describing the factors that put individuals at risk, ecological factors are significant and wide-ranging. They include chaotic and disorganized family life, shifting economic climates, cultural insensitivity, racism, sexism, ageism, and poverty.

Conclusions

Much more needs to be said about the ecological challenges to counseling in a world of cultural and racial diversity. Suffice it to say here that a growing awareness of ecological issues—whether framed in physical, social, economic, or moral terms—is compelling in its affirmation that the form and substance of counseling and of the problems persons bring to counselors are the products of complex transactions between individual perceptions and behavioral responses to the ecologies or ecological transitions people experience and manifest. Individual behavior does not occur in a social vacuum nor only as a function of mechanisms internal to the individual.

A major premise of such perspectives is that persons of different racial and cultural backgrounds and traditions are likely to be exposed to different ecologies, environments, life spaces, and opportunity structures. The forms and effects of such ecological contexts are mediated by cultural and racial issues, gender, and socioeconomic factors.

As a function of what transactions between people and their environments mean in terms of reinforcements, perceptions, self-esteem, knowledge, opportunities, and related matters, the needs for and processes of counseling need to vary across subpopulations and settings.

Both Britain and the United States are nations of cultural diversity and pluralism in which a mosaic of values, work ethics, worldviews, communication patterns, and meaning systems affect the behaviors of its populations. In turn, culturally sensitive counselors and the use of cross-cultural techniques become fundamental requirements for effective counseling. Draguns (1981) contended that such counseling is "not counseling as usual." In a general summation of advice to cross-cultural counselors and by extrapolation to counselors with clients whose ecological contexts are different because of variance in cultural and racial characteristics, Draguns stated, "be prepared to adapt you techniques...to the cultural background of the client; communicate acceptance of and respect for the client in terms that are intelligible and meaningful within his or her frame of reference; and be open to the possibility of more direct intervention in the life of the client than the traditional ethos of the counseling profession would dictate or permit" (p. 11). Such advice affirms that cultural and racial diversity and the variance in ecological issues with which people live and to which they respond are not benign, but instead must be central to the conceptions and practice of counseling in Great Britain and in the United States. Within the challenges of ecological issues, counselors can serve as maximizers of opportunities; as interpreters or translators of the relationships between environments and new and freer developmental trajectories; as providers and classifiers of relevant and accurate information; as support systems by which persons can acquire insight into their own stereotypes and irrational beliefs that have acted as brakes on their mobility; as stimuli to the use of strategies by which to increase their feelings of power and self-efficacy; as providers of psychoeducational processes by which persons can learn skills—e.g., assertiveness, anger management, conflict resolution, stress reduction, decision making—of pertinence to their mastery of a purposeful life transcending the bounds of ecologies and life spaces; and, as mentors and guides to balancing cultural pride and cultural adaptation.

References

Aponte, H. (1979). Family therapy and the community. In M.S. Gibbs, J.R. Lachenmeyer, & J. Sigal (Eds.), *Community psychology: Theoretical and empirical approaches.* New York: Gardner Press.

Bellak, R.N., Madsen, R., Sullivan, W., Swidler, A., & Tipton, S. (1985). *Habits of the heart; Individualism and commitment in American life.* New York: Harper & Row.

Blocker, O.H. (1987). *The professional counselor.* New York: Macmillan.

Bronfenbrenner, V. (1979). *The ecology of human development.* Cambridge, MA: Harvard University Press.

Clark, L.A. (1987). Mutual relevance of mainstreams and cross-cultural psychology. *Journal of Consulting and Clinical Psychology, 55*(4), 461–470.

Draguns, J.G. (1981). Counseling across cultures: Common themes and distinct approaches. In P.P. Pedersen, J.G. Draguns, W.J. Lonner, & J.E. Trimble (Eds.), *Counseling across cultures* (chapter 1). Honolulu: University of Hawaii Press.

Durkhheim, E. (1951). *Suicide.* New York: Free Press.

Hayghe, H. (1986, February). Rise in mothers' labor force participation includes these with young children. *Monthly Labor Review,* pp. 43–45.

Herr, E.L. (1989). *Counseling in a dynamic society: Opportunities and challenges.* Alexandria, VA: American Association for Counseling and Development.

Hines, P., & Boyd-Franklin, N. (1982). Black families. In M. McGoldrick, J.K. Pearce, & J. Giordano (Eds.), *Ethnicity and family therapy* (pp. 84–107). New York: Guilford Press.

Perry, L. (1982). Special populations: The demands of diversity. In E.L. Herr & N.M. Pinson (Eds.), *Foundations for policy guidance and counseling.* Falls Church, VA: American Personnel and Guidance Association.

Platt, S. (1984). Unemployment and suicidal behavior: A review of the literature. *Social Science Medicine, 19,* 93–115.

Platt, J., & Kreitman, N. (1985). Parasuicide and unemployment among men in Edinburgh, 1968–1982. *Psychological Medicine, 15,* 113–123.

Robins, L.N., & Kulbak, P.A. (1988). Chapter 13. In A.J. Frances & R.E. Hale (Eds.),

Review psychiatry, Volume 7 (pp. 289–306). Washington DC: American Psychiatric Press.

Robinson, B.E., Rowland, B.H., & Coleman, M. (1986). Marital and family therapy: A decade review. *Journal of Marriage & the Family, 42*(4), 239–259.

Spiegel, J. (1982). An ecological model of ethnic families. Chapter 2. In M. McGoldrick, J.K. Pearce, & J. Giordano (Eds.), *Ethnicity and family therapy* (pp. 31–54). New York: Guilford Press.

Sue, D.W. (1978). Eliminating cultural oppression in counseling: Toward a general theory. *Journal of Counseling Psychology, 25*, 419–428.

Sue, D., & Sue, J. (1987). Cultural factors in the clinical assessment of Asian Americans. *Journal of Consulting and Clinical Psychology, 55*(4) 479–487.

Turkington, C. (1983). Lifetime of fear may be legacy of latchkey children. *APA Monitor, 14*, 19.

Wasserman, I.M. (1984). The influence of economic business cycles on United States suicide rates. *Suicide and Life-Threatening Behavior, 14*, 143–156.

Webster: New universal unabridged dictionary (2nd ed.). (1983). New York: Dorsett & Baker.

ECOLOGICAL INTERRELATEDNESS: A GLOBAL COUNSELING PERSPECTIVE

John A. McFadden

In recent years at numerous conferences at international, national, and regional levels, economic development experts have stressed the urgency of maintaining the concept of "sustainable development." However, problems of environmental degradation are becoming more serious daily, particularly in developing countries. It is now apparent that ecologically sound environmental management practices should be developed to stimulate self-propelling momentum to ensure and secure the livelihood of humankind and provide food, fuel, fiber, purified water, and dependable shelter. As counselors, we, therefore, need to design a counseling environment that prevents environmental mismanagement and enables families, groups, and communities to discuss immediate ecological problems related to the security of their livelihood in the context of managing basic life support systems.

I believe that we need, for this purpose, a global grid of conservation entities committed to and organized by educational institutions to encourage ecological awareness and sustainable development in village schools, community groups, as well as colleges and universities. In such entities counselors can play an important part in disseminating appropriate information and offering guidance. Without such commitment, I am afraid the plea for peoples' participation in programs designed to foster development and avoid environmental destruction may remain merely a slogan. The African food crisis, for example, underlines the urgency of harmonizing ecological and agricultural rehabilitation plans. Unless this happens, the quality of life in Third World countries will further deteriorate, leading to an increased influx of environmental refugees in relief camps, presently witnessed in the Sudan and other states that are totally dependent on donations given primarily by Western societies.

Anderson (1981) defined ecology as a study of the relationship between organisms and their environment. The term *environment* is often used to refer to the physio-chemical parameters of the habitat where organisms live. Species, however, do not exist in isolation from one another and, therefore, their natural environment includes other organisms. Such biotic dimensions of the environment define the ecological components of various disciplines.

An organism and the environment to which it is adapted are inseparable ecological units. The ultimate goal in ecological science, the understanding of why living systems exist in their observed form, and why functional relationships occur, can basically be answered by a holistic approach: Such systems require a functional approach between the parts and the whole system that is analogous to what counselors must understand in order to deal with problems of pluralistic societies in the United States and the United

Kingdom as well as intervening in those social problems brought about by global ecological deterioration.

The aim of this presentation is to highlight the interrelatedness between humans and their environment by describing the relationship of diverse cultures that need to be viewed from a global perspective. In addition, this paper will argue that different cultures appeal differently to various groups of people, and that the notion that the environment is something to be conquered and controlled is highly questionable. The impact of such a stance is counterproductive to the environment in the world today. In the process of striving to conquer nature, humans have utilized various techniques created by modern technology, which has resulted in the current global ecological decline. I shall develop this position based on studies conducted on the environment and related cultural issues within tropical environments. I will draw conclusions indicating why we urgently need to respond to the situation with immediacy to deal with this worsening transnational problem. Furthermore, the paper will show the role of counseling professionals in helping people from diverse backgrounds make transitions from the traditional myth of controlling the environment to a different level of learning to cope with and respect nature. Finally, this presentation is designed to urge professional counselors to pull their efforts together to assist individuals, couples, families, and community groups to deal with the effects of problems caused by current environmental destabilization and deterioration and to work toward common ground to abate further worsening of our worldwide environmental pollution.

The Concept of One World

Although the concept of "one world" has been a popular idea among writers and politicians for some time, it did not become a visual reality until the space age scientific accomplishments of both the United States and the Soviet Union. The astronauts and cosmonauts on U.S. and U.S.S.R. space missions were extremely impressed by the beauty and isolation of our planet during their flights and space-walk experiences. They saw its magnificent greens, blues, and browns, as Southwick (1985) noted, surrounded by a swirling atmosphere of moisture-laden clouds. These impressions bordered on a religious experience for some, particularly U.S. astronauts. This was especially true among the Apollo cress as they journeyed from the life-giving earth to the lifeless moon, through contrasts that were obvious and strong.

In more than 25 years of human activity in space, orbital flights have become almost routine. The uses of space science, industry, and human performance in space have greatly expanded and changed the impressions of those on the surface of the globe as well. The astronauts of the space shuttle "Challenger" in 1983 reported that they were utterly shocked to see the amount of pollution surrounding the earth. As reported by Southwick, Commander Paul Weitz remarked, "Unfortunately, this world is becoming a grey planet....Our environment apparently is going downhill....We are fouling our own nest."

This realization may seem trivial to most of us on earth. But we have all experienced air and water pollution as well as the loss of a remembered childhood view of a field, creek, forest, or pond to urban growth or suburban development. What is new and frightening to us today is the fact that these changes are now clearly visible from space, that they are affecting the entire planet. It was only one quarter of a century ago when the Apollo astronauts witnessed the beauty of our planet from their spacecraft. Today, less than three decades later, we are told that this beautiful and only life-sustaining planet we know, our home in space, is on the verge of disaster. What do we do? Who is going to provide solutions to the problem? Nations, organizations, professionals, individuals, all have a share to contribute. We as professional counselors within Western societies must be able to divorce ourselves from regional, ethnic, and racial prejudices and make available our knowledge, experiences, and resources to those who need them. We must be able to convince our society of the importance of these issues and help to set examples that serve humankind. Our contribution should be unique in providing information, support, and direction for efforts by which to meet the essential needs of our own kind.

A Global Ecology

The scientific facts that come pouring at us from all directions highlight the importance of a global ecology that encompasses many components. These facts describe an accumulation of local and regional environmental mismanagements often considered trivial until they assume global importance in the form of acid rains, soil erosion, coastal pollution, and global warming—obvious signs of the downhill trend of our environmental conditions that the astronauts noted from space. Other events in global ecology can be of such planetary impact that they may not be easily observed at the local level. New approaches and techniques may be required to evaluate such hidden changes.

It is important to understand that environmental problems do not stop at national boundaries. In the past decade, we in the Western hemisphere and in nations in other parts of the world have come to recognize the urgency of international efforts to protect our common environments. In fact, government concern over trends in population, resources, and environment is not new. For example, Barney's (1980) study on these issues by the Federal Commissions and Planning Boards extends back at least 70 years. Earlier studies, however, tended to view each of the aforementioned issues as separate, without relating one to the other, limiting inquiries to the borders of the U.S. or the U.K. and dwelling mainly on the short-term future. What is new in more recent studies is a growing cognizance of the interdependence of population, resources, environment, and nations. The studies based on such notions indicate, as well, the increasing potential for global problem interrelatedness. Environmental, resource, and population stresses are intensifying and will increasingly determine the quality of human life on our planet. These trends are already severe enough to deny many millions of people their basic needs for food, shelter, health, and jobs, or any hope for improvement in their circumstances. At the same time, the earth's carrying capacity—the ability of biological systems to provide resources for human needs—is diminishing. The trends reflected in the Global 2000 Study (Barney, 1980) suggest a progressive degradation and impoverishment of the earth's natural resource base. In view of such predictions, it is imperative that professional assistance be provided to help society better prepare for such dangers. It is this concern that we need to address today. I am sure we concur that facing this huge challenge cannot be left totally to environmentalists or engineers. The time has come that counselors must stand firm in their thoughts and performance behind efforts striving to prevent and possibly roll back environmental degradation. Tackling such phenomenal problems requires transnational approaches and paradigms that treat all societies symmetrically and respect ethnic and other differentials as givens. We must understand that there is no superior-inferior relationship between cultures. Differences between cultures and practices should not be assumed to be differences in quality but must be accepted as differences in approach, geographical position, and cultural heritage.

Counseling in a Global Ecology

McFadden's (1976) stylistic dimensions of counseling model, which presents a framework for counselors to provide effective delivery services for minorities and the disadvantaged, can be cited as an example of a model for counseling in a pluralistic society. This model originally emerged out of a need to assist and train Black people in the United States. In recent years, however, the model has had extended applicability to other oppressed individuals throughout the United States. It has, for example, been applied to poor Caucasians in the Appalachian Mountains and to other economically disadvantaged groups. It was implemented in various national and international counseling conferences. The model has been used in training experiences at military counseling workshops in Washington, DC, and has proved to be quite promising in that respect. These and other applications of professional and leadership development seminars indicate the possible adaptability of the framework in both educational and other community settings of multicultural societies. With some additional elements, such paradigms can be shaped to fit the needs of counselors in their attempts to deal with cross-cultural problems caused by environmental deterioration under scrutiny here.

A number of responses to global resource, environment, and population issues began to appear in the 1970s. According to Southwick (1985), heightened international concern was reflected in conferences convened by the United Nations on Human Environment (1972); Population (1974); Food (1974); Human Settlements (1976); Water (1977); Desertification (1977); Science and Technology for Development (1979); and New and Renewable Sources of Energy (August 1981). However, given the urgency, scope and complexity of the challenges before us, the efforts in process around the world do not seem to answer the call. An era of unprecedented global cooperation and commitment by everyone is essential.

The necessary changes to bring about an abatement in global environmental decline and deterioration go beyond the capability of any single nation. Nations together can exert important and exemplary steps toward initiating momentum to minimize the trend. Because of the preeminent position of Western nations as producers and consumers of food and energy, our efforts to conserve soil, farmlands, and energy resources are of national as well as global importance. We can avoid polluting our own environment, and we must take care that we do not degrade the global environment. Counselors must be committed to teaching those who do not know that the effects of their activities will endanger the existence of the human race and at the same time be prepared, as previously stated, to expose those who know that the effects of their activities are dangerous and yet pay minimal attention to reality. There is no time to stand on the side and shrug one's shoulders and remain indifferent.

We should expand our collaboration beyond our borders, including both developed and developing nations, in a networking spirit with a base of justice. Hundreds of millions of the world's people are trapped in a condition of abject poverty and degradation and need the professional help of counselors not only in schools but in all walks of life. People at the margins of existence must take cropland, grazing land, and fuel where they can find it, regardless of the effects upon the earth's resource base. Sustainable economic development, coupled with environmental protection and resource management, is essential. Equally important to all professionals in dealing with the problem of environmental degradation is a better understanding of the appropriate, effective, and timely responses to such global problems as the buildup of life-threatening gases and residual particles from our factories into the atmosphere that continue to menace the human species on a massive scale.

If present trends continue unchecked, it is predicted that the world in the year 2000 will be not only more crowded, but also more polluted, less stable ecologically, and more vulnerable to disruption than the world in which we live today. Serious stresses on population, resources, and environment are clearly visible ahead of us. Despite greater material production, the people of the world will be poorer in many ways than they are today. For hundreds of millions of the desperately poor, the outlook for food and other necessities of life will be no better; for many, it may worsen. In many ways, the major factor responsible for increasing pollution since the end of World War II is the intensified effect of numerous faulty technological approaches coupled with professional apathy to safeguard societal well-being (Nader, 1970).

Professional Responsibility

Much has been said about the responsibility of professionals. For example, lawyers have obligations to their clients, but they also have some conflicting obligations to the legal system within which they serve and to the general citizenry that the legal system purports to protect. Doctors owe responsibility to their patients, but they are also linked to medical science and the general public's health and well-being. Many engineers have corporate employers or clients to whom they owe their loyalty, but they also are required with varying degrees of compulsion to honor codes of ethics, which mandate that they never sacrifice the health and safety of others to suit the whims of their clients. And so it goes with all professionals whose careers have developed from a tradition of applying to problems independent judgment based on expertise and education.

But scientists place themselves in a different category. They are bound to search for facts. They are compelled to discover the truth in their respective disciplines, and, in a sense, view the truth as their client. Unfortunately, too many scientists are content to rest their commitment to social responsibility on this truism. According to environmentalists, professional societies in general as well as engineering and other scientific societies in particular continue to issue vague pronouncements about moral and professional responsibilities. Scientists and other experts who deal with the discovery of facts often feel that they possess the means to conquer nature. In view of what has resulted from some technological practices, one may question whether science, although it provides many of the tools important to modern civilization, is the only answer to controlling the operation of our planet.

Select professionals, for example, are among the first to know about industrial dumping of mercury or fluoride sludge into waterways, defectively designed automobiles, or undisclosed adverse effects of prescription drugs and pesticides. They can be the first to grasp the technical means of preventing existing product or pollution hazards.

Unfortunately, they are frequently the last to speak out, much less to refuse to be recruited to support or perform acts of corporate or governmental negligence or predation. A good example is the nearly 25-year collusion by U.S. automobile companies against the development and marketing of exhaust control systems (Hilton, 1976), which represents a tragic spoiling of the environment by the industries' defiance, to say nothing of the cynical and knowing violation of American antitrust laws by lawyers and high corporate officials. A prime foundation of professionalism should have been sufficient independence to pursue a course that could save lives, secure rights, and preserve property unjustly imperiled by greedy employers. It must then be the responsibility of counselors and other helping professionals to face the challenge of these malaises without wavering from the truth or being blinded by cultural and other prejudices.

Transnational Counseling

As counselors and psychologists, we should understand the global population distribution patterns since the 1940s. According to Raven (1985), during the past 35 years, well over 2 billion people have been added in the less developed countries (LCDs) alone. About 90% of such countries lie wholly or partially within the tropics, a relationship that is very important for us to understand as we begin to tackle the issue of transnational counseling. Simultaneously, there are expansions of pressures in all corners of the globe due to starvation in the LCDs, a tide of immigration to the North/Western worlds, terrorist threats, and drug-related problems from which nations can never divorce themselves. These problems hit Western society hard. Thus, we cannot seclude ourselves in attempts to solve only national problems. We have to develop broader multicultural and cross-cultural counseling paradigms that address national issues in the context of international problems. We also must be prepared to find new techniques to address international issues related to environmental degradation, population explosion, and economic malfunctions partly generated by ecological destabilization or downturn.

The developed countries, with less than a quarter of the people in the world, as Raven reports, enjoy an average per capita income of more than $9,000 and control some 80% of the global economy. In stark contrast, the less developed countries, with a far too small per capita income, control only 17.6% of the world's wealth. Hence, counselors must be in a position to pursue an independent course to help not only their multicultural nationals but also to encourage Western society as a whole, and the U.S.-U.K. in particular, to help the Third World meet its astronomical economical challenges and related political problems by providing a cooperative basis for remedial projects.

For example, the destruction of the tropical forests in the world today is so extensive, so devastating, so irrevocable that humanity may soon lose its richest, most diverse, and most valuable biotic resources. As a consequence, life will lose much of its capability for continued evolution. Many groups of the higher vertebrates (mammals, birds, reptiles) will be especially affected. The economic, aesthetic, and cultural losses to future generations will be incalculable.

This damage may not be visible to Western scientists, educators, and counselors for the tropics are far away—hot and humid places about which we know very little and have been taught even less. To most of us in the U.S. and Britain, the word "tropics" itself conjures up a picture of pristine nature, mysterious, and yet marvelous; of great apes and elephants, of orchids and palms.

The horrendous destruction of nature over the past half century—the critical reason for the widespread concern among biologists and environmentalists—has often been conveniently ignored or belittled by politicians and the world media. The realistic ecological picture today and its long-range implications are very grim indeed.

Those of us who take pride in being environmentally enlightened have been teaching pollution control and contour ploughing, nature preservation, and other land ethics mostly with reference to our own temperate biota. What concern we may have had for the tropics was rarely based on reality. In our comfortable unawareness, those bush lands and their wildlife seemed so safe, so infinite, and so insulated from destruction that we rarely worried about their fate. The underdevelopment, the innocence of their illiterate populations, and the endemic tropical plagues like malaria and yellow fever that kept their populations well in check seemed certain to offer them ample protection.

Many well-meaning Western advisors and humanitarians have been misled by the luxuriance of the tropical forests. How many times have they announced that the answer to world hunger lies in the forests' sustained agricultural utilization? Yet, ignorance of the ecology in such cases is fatal. As Professor Chang (1970) of the University of Hawaii explained, despite their lushness, annual grasses such as wheat, rye, barley, and rice in tropical regions have relatively low agricultural productivity compared to those species found in the cool temperate climates. He argues that this is due to changes in the bioclimatic processes. Thus, the tropics introduce a climatically determined paradox. Biologically, they are rich beyond belief, but in many significant ways they are agriculturally poor. Among others, counselors bear the burden of enlightening those who, either knowingly or unknowingly, are engaged in destroying the habitat.

Studies show some bright light amid all this destruction. According to Iltis (1985), advances have been made in some of the South American countries—Bolivia, Brazil, Equador, and Venezuela—where nearly 12 million hectares of tropical forest have been placed under protection. But most of these important projects, in Cooke's (1984) view, exist on paper only.

We are experiencing both hypocrisy and tragedy: hypocrisy because these geographic-economic factors are well known but too inconvenient to be accepted; and tragedy because what the underdeveloped countries need now more than anything else are freely available and medically safe population control measures on the one hand, and peace and freedom from economic manipulation and exploitation by the overdeveloped countries on the other. On both of these counts, the U.S., Britain, and the Western European countries directly influence a move against measures detrimental to the environment anywhere on the globe without being ambiguous, vacillating, or self-serving.

Counselors should be engaged in processes that aim at accomplishing personal and institutional change. By providing new or additional information about ways to help people succeed in their chosen goals in life, counselors must offer society an opportunity to rethink assumptions and rearrange means concerning personal interaction with the surrounding environment. In helping society to come to terms with difficulties, in organizing work and other conflicts related to the environment, counselors are expected to be in a position to deal with resulting cognitive and emotional changes. Counselors have to play a part in society in developing purposeful action aimed at resolving the specific challenge of environmental decline by involving themselves in efforts to enlighten and bring about positive change. As counselors, we need not wait for the affected to appear before us for help, but rather we must stretch out to help those who are confused and discouraged by the ecological decline and assist them to adjust to changing situations and develop possible preventive measures.

We are aware that the forces opposing a rational solution to the ever-expanding ecological problems are extreme and influential. This influence has been evidenced in the sabotage and death of the 1970 formation of "Earth Day" (Iltis, 1985), which was introduced to remind us to dedicate ourselves to a biologically sane world. Now, 19 years later, as Iltis argues, this profound intellectual revolution is all but forgotten, obviously sabotaged by the system, that is, by administrative officials and by heavily subsidized and carefully orchestrated campaigns of the media and their corporate allies and shareholders, who continue to obscure the real dangers in neglecting the world's most dangerous problem, pollution.

We need only point out that the special anniversary issue of *Time* magazine entitled, "The Most Amazing 60 Years in History," published October 5, 1983, only minimally raised or illustrated in its 168 pages of text and lavish pictures, information on environmental problems, on "Earth Day," on the expanding use of DDT in Third World countries after being legally outlawed for use among Western societies, or on increasing extinction of species due to pollution; in generic terms, there was a surprisingly limited mention of any environmental issues.

While corporations exploit and their political associates run interference for dubious economic aims, we must keep in mind that equally responsible for many of the biological maladies around the world are poverty, hunger, and ignorance—in other words, the destruction of millions of trees, coupled with the need to feed billions of mouths that totally depend on the land. For example, although people of the tropics do need more protein, they need birth control even more because the food-versus-population race will not be won by furthering the immaculate misconception of raising more food through clearing additional fields and ploughing them or by draining more wetlands. We are running out of these resources, and the population bomb keeps on ticking. Here is the most important juncture where we as professional helpers enter in order to assist society in making important decisions.

We must impress upon our students and clients these facts:

- The world endurance is finite;
- There are too many mouths to feed and vast needs to satisfy; and
- The actual collision between resource demands (including clean air, food supply, and other necessities) and the ability to attain them continues to show a mismatch and imbalance.

This, in fact, is the most fundamental, and nearly insoluble, problem that continues to challenge us as professionals. The challenge has to be met by individuals from all walks of life, disregarding racial, cultural, ethnic, and regional diversities. The impact of this challenge affects every human being—families, communities, nations, regions, and the international community at large. The time is now, ladies and gentlemen, to tighten our belts, abandon our differences, and coalesce to confront this ever-expanding challenge of environmental decline by helping our kind to steer our ship, the earth, to a safer ground. Thank you and together we stand, as "sticks in a bundle."

References

Anderson, J.M. (1981). *Ecology for environmental sciences: Biosphere, ecosystem and man.* New York: Wiley.

Barney, O. (1980). *The global 2000 report to the president: Entering the twenty-first century,* Vol. 2. Washington, DC: U.S. Government Printing Office.

Chang, J. (1970). Potential photosynthesis and crop productivity. *Annals of the Association of American Geographers, 60,* 92–101.

Cooke, R. (1985). Interfacing with the elements: Man and biogeochemical cycles. In C. Southwick (Ed.), *Global ecology.* Sunderland, MA: Sinauer Associates.

Hilton, A.M. (Ed.), (1976). *Against population and hunger: Notes toward a new world.* Oslo, Norway: Universitetsforlaget.

Iltis, H.H. (1985). *Tropical forests: What will be their fate?* New York: Sinauer Associates.

McFadden, J. (1976). Stylistic dimensions of counseling Blacks. *Journal of Non-White Concerns, 5*(1), 23–28.

Nader, R. (1970). Professional responsibility. In A.M. Hilton (Ed.), *Against population and hunger* (pp. 19–24). Oslo, Norway: Universitetsforlaget.

Raven, P.H. (1985). Third World in the global future. In C. Southwick (Ed.), *Global ecology* (pp. 307–312). Sunderland, MA: Sinauer Associates.

Southwick, C.H. (Ed.). (1985). *Global ecology.* Sunderland, MA: Sinauer Associates.

CROSS-CULTURAL COUNSELING ISSUES AND THE EDUCATION OF MINORITIES IN THE UNITED STATES

Sara E. Melendez

Dr. Herr has done an excellent job of describing the issues involved in counseling members of minority groups in the United States given our current human ecological system. At the crux of all the issues is the fact that, as Dr. Herr stated: "...persons of different racial or cultural backgrounds are likely to experience habitats, life spaces, environments, resource availability, and ecological contexts that are in fact different because of their cultural or racial characteristics." This fact is critical in a country where almost one quarter of the population are members of minority groups and where, by the year 2015, it is expected that one third will be so, where public school children speak over 100 languages.

For 5 ½ years, until December 1988, I worked with the Office of Minority Concerns at the American Council on Education. The office was charged with planning projects, research, and policy to improve opportunities for people from racial and ethnic minority backgrounds to achieve a college education and to increase the numbers of minority faculty and administrators.

Ecological Contexts Differ in Cultural and Racial Terms

One of the problems we faced during the last 8 years was that too many people in positions of power did not understand the extent to which it is still true in the United States that people's habitats, life spaces, environments, resource availability, and ecological contexts are different because of their cultural or racial characteristics. This was evident in policies that implied that all we have to do is prohibit discrimination and let everybody compete on equal terms for jobs, educational opportunities, and government contracts. One of the pet phrases was that we only had to guarantee opportunity, not results.

What was not understood was that the ecological context, or situational circumstances, still shape the possibilities for choice, the information that people receive about opportunities, and their ability to avail themselves of the opportunities. Merely prohibiting discrimination does not prepare people for full participation. This lack of understanding by those in power, and even by many in our colleges and universities, has given rise to a population of students on our campuses who cannot understand why we have programs to assist Blacks, Hispanics, and Native Americans, and not them. They believe that because their parents have had to work hard to put them through college they should have the same rights to special programs as do people from minority backgrounds.

We have not helped them understand the compounding effects of race and ethnicity on poverty. And we have not helped them understand it because there are still many on the faculty and in the administration and in counseling who do not understand it themselves. This lack of understanding exists among those who work with children as well as those in higher education.

Many teachers and counselors of elementary and secondary school children cannot understand why so few parents show up at parent-teacher conferences, or why so few go to parents' meetings, or why some do not even appear when they are asked to go to see the teacher or principal. They interpret this as lack of interest or aspiration. They then interpret the children's behaviors as based in lack of motivation and support from parents.

Minority Members Judged by Middle-Class, Western-European Standards

Unfortunately too often, even now, when minority parents interact with any government agency, they are judged by the middle-class, Anglo, or Western-European standards of the service providers and the agency. Of course, often the parents are found wanting. Let me give you an example.

A young Puerto Rican mother in a town in Connecticut went before a family court judge for a hearing on whether to return her children to her. They had been removed from her home for neglect. This is very common in that town with Puerto Rican parents. Parents have been charged with neglect for leaving small children with their older siblings, who are also children, or for not sending them to school. This young mother was a single parent of a couple of children, living on welfare.

The judge declared that he did not see any reason why the children should be returned to their mother because she obviously was not interested enough in the proceedings to look at him or anybody else; she had never been to see the children in the weeks that they had been in a foster home; and she had never even telephoned them during that time.

This woman was lucky, because there was a Hispanic volunteer from a community-based agency there with her who intervened and explained to the judge what was going on. She explained that for many poor and working-class Puerto Ricans it was a sign of respect not to look at anyone in authority, such as parents, judges, teachers, or bosses, so the young woman was showing respect for the judge and the attorneys by not looking at them. The reason she had not visited the children was because they had been placed in a home far from where she lived, she could not reach it on public transportation, and she had no automobile. Finally, she explained that she had not called the children because she spoke no English and the foster parents spoke no Spanish.

I wish I could tell you that this kind of cross-cultural miscommunication or conflict were history. Unfortunately, it is still going on in many cities of the United States. The incident I just told you about happened last year in a town where about one third of the residents are Hispanics.

Techniques Cannot Ignore Cultural or Racial Differences

Dr. Herr stated that "...the assumptions and techniques of counseling have frequently ignored such cultural or racial differences or treated them as benign." We must include languages among the factors ignored. This is also true of the techniques of teaching—children from minority backgrounds have been treated as deficient. Remediation, counseling, and other services have traditionally been based on the deficit model. Part of the educational and counseling process has always been an attempt to assimilate these children, make them eradicate every trace of difference. Many teachers and counselors become frustrated at what they judge as a refusal to assimilate—the children's maintenance of the native language and cultural behaviors.

In higher education, we find that in the late 1960s many laws, policies, and types of funding were enacted for redressing past wrongs of discrimination and exclusion on the basis of race and ethnicity. This has had some fascinating results. First, the numbers and percentages of Blacks and Hispanics enrolled in colleges and universities increased dramatically. At the peak of enrollments, Blacks were going to college at rates indistinguishable from Whites, and Hispanics were going at rates higher than any other group. Although many students did not graduate, many did, and the number of degree holders increased significantly also. This made it obvious that an important factor in the low numbers of enrollments and degrees earned had been arbitrary, exclusionary practices.

Opening the doors the first few years was limited to just that. Nothing changed in the teaching-learning relationship and, in fact, not much was done directly to help students survive in their new environment. It was more or less a sink-or-swim approach, and many students sank.

When higher education officials realized that they may have to do something besides just admit minority students, they implemented support programs such as academic support, counseling, and cultural activities. But these efforts were not more than offering college students the same types of interventions that had been attempted in the public schools. These interventions amounted to an assimilation program, or making the students over into White, middle-class, European-culture-oriented people. The task was to change the students to make them fit the institutions. The deficit model ran rampant. Very little, if anything, was done to tailor the programs to the students' learning styles or cultural backgrounds. By and large, higher education institutions took their traditional approaches and used them with the new population, adding components on orientation to college, and things like budgeting and study skills. Most of these approaches were not looked at from a cultural perspective.

Nevertheless, many such programs worked for many students. The number of degrees awarded to Blacks and Hispanics continued to increase until about 1981. But then we had several years of decline for Blacks and a slowed rate of growth for Hispanics, even though we had not yet reached parity.

In the last 2 or 3 years, with the decline in the traditional college-going cohort due to the declining birth rate for Whites, and the increase in the proportion of the population that is Black, Hispanic, or Asian, colleges and universities, federal, state, and local governments, and business and industry leaders have been paying attention to the demographics and talking about the need to increase the educational attainment of minority groups.

In the last couple of years, almost every higher education association has appointed a commission, task force, or advisory committee to study the problem and recommend strategies. The National Governors Association held a conference a few years ago, and issued a report on "youth at risk." Also, a great many foundations and corporate philanthropy groups have placed a priority on programs for minorities.

Recommendations for Action

What is most interesting about the new awareness is that people are beginning to realize that perhaps it is time to look at our institutions to see whether there is something about the way they go about their business that needs to change if we are to do a better job of educating minority students. Even as mainstream an organization as the American Council on Education has recommended that we look at our teaching and counseling and recruitment strategies to see whether they need changing to accommodate the new populations.

I think it is interesting that there is a surprising amount of agreement among government, corporate, foundation, or association reports on some of the things that must be done. They all recommend paying more attention to the total needs of families of small children, offering better preschool education, and improving the quality of counseling.

In terms of counseling, the fact is that many minority children in inner-city schools don't see much of guidance counselors. Counselors in such schools often cannot do much more than fill out forms and, therefore, spend time only on the students who are creating the most problems for the school. Well-behaved children, even though they may not be learning, are often missed in the counseling process.

Too often, still, minority students are overrepresented in special education programs and, more often than White students, are labeled as learning disabled, mentally retarded, and emotionally disturbed. Now, it is entirely possible that given the additional stresses on their lives as described by Dr. Herr that a disproportionate number of minority students would exhibit problems. But given the state of the counseling system in the large city school districts, we have to exercise a certain amount of healthy skepticism and do whatever may be necessary to ensure that the process is not mislabeling and misplacing children.

Other recommendations have dealt with paying attention to cognitive and learning styles in the design of both counseling and teaching strategies. Another recommendation that seems very basic but is lacking in many schools and on many campuses is coordination between the counseling and academic programs. I taught for 3 years in an elementary school in New York City. Not once during that time did a counselor visit my classroom to observe students in their learning environment.

On too many college campuses counselors never talk to faculty and vice versa. Faculty often do not know what support services are available to students, and students are often left floundering. This makes the experience difficult for all students, but for students from minority backgrounds, who are often first-generation students and have no other resources to turn to, it can make the difference between success or failure.

The American Council on Education issued a handbook to assist institutions of higher education in their efforts to increase minority participation. It is called *Minorities on Campus: A Handbook for Enhancing Diversity.* It is a practical manual describing strategies that have been used with some success on campuses around the country.

The book expresses several overarching principles. A very important principle is that programs to improve minority participation must be central to the mission of the college or university. The issue can no longer be seen as merely one of fairness and equity, but one of centrality to the well-being of society and the country's ability to maintain its position of leadership and competitiveness.

Success will require leadership from the top, from the president and all the top-level administrators. They must use all their leadership skills to mobilize the energy, resources, and creativity of others on campus working toward shared goals. They must require accountability and reward accomplishment and penalize its lack.

Programs must be comprehensive and well coordinated, and they must be seen as long-term efforts. The situation is not likely to be turned around overnight, or even over a year or two. Finally, some efforts will require funding, which may require revisiting and reordering an institution's priorities.

Counselors and counseling are integral to the efforts to increase the ability of minorities in the United States to find their niche in our country's human ecological system. But it is important for counseling to be sensitive to the cultural issues that Dr. Herr has presented.

Because counselors, probably more than most other professionals with whom minority children and young adults come in contact, are sensitive to cultural issues, they can be a valuable resource to school systems, colleges and universities, and other service providing agencies in helping them understand these issues and tailor their services accordingly.

ECOLOGICAL ISSUES WORKSHOPS

Part I concludes with two papers presented in the workshops at Brunel University that address ecological issues as part of the challenges of cultural and racial diversity to counseling in Britain and the United States. These papers take a somewhat different tack than the plenary papers just presented.

In the first paper Ian R. Owen, a social therapist in London, draws ideas from anthropology and applies them to Carl Rogers's client-centered therapy in an effort to widen the awareness of therapists. The author highlights some areas in counseling where greater awareness is required to create a holistic counseling philosophy and to improve the ethics, power sharing, efficacy, and appropriateness of therapy. The intention is to show that culture clash inevitably occurs between all clients and therapists. This paper describes one way to understanding clients' lives by understanding personality type and culture.

In the second paper, C. Scully Stikes, an assistant chancellor of student affairs at the University of Wisconsin-Milwaukee, examines a model of counseling that he believes can be adapted for use in all cultures and subcultures of a pluralistic society. The author believes it to be an authentic model responsive to comprehensive human needs that can effect strategies for positive self-direction for individuals in any society.

The Application of Some Ideas From Anthropology to Counseling, Therapy, and Cross-Cultural Counseling

Ian R. Owen

The starting point for this discussion is to take three concepts from anthropology, the study of people in cultures, and to apply these to highlight areas in counseling. The three concepts are *etic, emic,* and *culture-bound.* This discussion takes the notion of cross-cultural counseling and states that when a therapist and client meet there is a cross-cultural communication taking place—regardless of the racial, educational, or socioeconomic similarities between the two parties. I wish to expand therapists' awareness by making this distinction: I propose that the therapist comes from a therapy tribe and the client comes from a lay person's suffering tribe. I also state that for therapy to be effective for clients, the therapy has to be wholly appropriate for each client. The discussion presented here calls for a holistic view of communication between people, that is, the use of methods, techniques, and therapy procedures between real people. Also I propose a reminder that human qualities are part of people's lives and that people are enmeshed in living culture.

The "Etic" Concept

An etic study, viewpoint, or understanding is one in which information is gathered according to preconceived notions and concepts, which were in force before the study was started. In counseling, this is fitting the client to the therapist's constructs. Such an etic approach in counseling produces pseudo client-centred therapy. In the worst case the therapist has only one style of working and doles out the same attitudes and approaches to all clients. Etic therapy is a theoretical science approach to counseling—it creates careful definitions and first principles on which to base its findings. Then it adds on other principles to the first principles.

I propose that culture clash in therapy and cross-cultural counseling is created by rigid etic philosophies. The various models, schools, or systems of counseling and therapy all propound a certain worldview. Medical models, psychological models, sociological models, spiritual models, moral models, or psychopharmacological models are all limited viewpoints.

I believe that such labeling in counseling can be the basis of prejudice on the part of the therapist. I think in therapy there can be an exploitation of the client by the more powerful therapist, although such an exploitation is unwitting or unconscious. I ask practitioners to reflect carefully on and give attention to the power play between themselves and their clients. Psychotherapy and counseling have their own "racism" and discrimination if they scapegoat some attitudes as being wrong, incorrect, or irrational.

The "Emic" Concept

An emic understanding or viewpoint is a subjective or phenomenological one. Viewing the world through the client's eyes is one of the avowed intentions of many therapists. But actually to take the time or be able to come to such an understanding is difficult. An emic understanding is one where the therapist has elicited the frameworks of meaning, classificatory schemes, and ideas of causation of the client. The therapist allows the client to define her problem to her own satisfaction. Such a distinction between emic and etic ways of working with clients was Carl Rogers's breakthrough and pioneering work (Rogers, 1951). To provide therapy for the *client's* needs, views, and experiences is paramount. I state that counseling needs to follow Rogers's lead and go beyond his work. I state that a truly client-centred therapist has a sensitivity to the needs of clients that enables the therapist to provide a variable content of therapy that is appropriate and designed for each client. Such appropriate therapy deals in terms of the subjectivity, psychodynamics, and self-healing mechanisms of the client and her social context.

Emic ways of working are the careful appreciation of the client and her words, energies, defense mechanisms, habits, and interests in enabling the client to enter therapeutic experiences. When the therapist takes the time to enter the client's world, then emic therapy begins. An emic approach is one that is phenomenological, subjective, emotional, existential, experiential, aetiological, philosophical, and ethical. In this approach therapists' interventions are such that the client can be enabled to make his or her own interventions. Some aspects of Milton Erickson's work (Hayley, 1973) and Freud's free association can be considered as emic. The work of David Grove (Grove & Panzer, 1989) is considered by this author to be particularly emic.

The Concept of Being "Culture-Bound"

A starting point of anthropology is a definition of the term *culture*. A metaphor for culture is to imagine a millipede. Briefly, an anthropologist regards individuals as the legs of a millipede. Each leg moves in accordance with the others. The anthropologist seeks to study the whole creature. The psychologist studies only each leg (Mars, personal communication, 1988).

Culture occurs at national, regional, local, and neighborhood levels. There are different influences on culture from economic, religious, financial, and political forces. There can be said to be cultures and cultural norms for men and women, the middle-aged, teenagers, or children.

Most therapies are American, and American psychotherapeutic evangelism plays a part in selling American therapies inside and outside the U.S.A. Philosophically and ethically I differentiate out of American therapies certain beliefs and attitudes that are assumed to be universal, right, and proper for psychotherapeutic and social change.

The horror (or the glory) of a "sales culture" (Douglas, 1978) is that Heinz tomato soup made in Turkey, from different ingredients than those used in other countries, tastes just the same as Heinz tomato soup made anywhere else. A mass "sales culture" destroys individuality and nonconformity. As there are Heinz, McDonald's, Coke, Dallas, and Dynasty—so there are the counseling and psychotherapy equivalents of these. The "sales culture" of counseling believes in **self-responsibility** and **pragmatism** as forces that **empower** the **individual. Technology** is king and **science** is queen in the quest to pour funds and attention into making everything in therapy known and safe. Therapy is based on influencing, persuading, and communicating. Personal **achievement** is everything in a fight to do the **latest** and most **effective** and **efficient** therapy. The cultural imperatives are to be **an extrovert** and **innovate** for innovation's sake. Sales culture is just one of a series of themes that need to be identified in therapy.

"Sales culture" breeds "sales" therapies. In a sales culture the therapist says: "I've got just the right therapy for you. Join my group. This therapy is growing quickly. It's new and scientifically proven to be effective in 8 out of 10 phobias. I teach you skills for use in the here and now. It gets straight to the parts of you that other therapies can't reach." And what the therapist says is met with approval from clients whose enculturation has led them to believe that failure means guilt and regret at missed opportunities, isolation, self-directed anger, and despair that they will never achieve their ambitions. The goals of therapy are defined as the achievement of spontaneity, intimacy, and having awareness in the present. Therapists are pragmatic, eclectic, and critical of other therapies in general.

Central to the holding of beliefs by people is how one group of people regard another people's beliefs. I define irrationality as being something you don't believe in. Hence rational thought, behavior, and justification are culture-bound. All cultures produce their own therapies; these could be called culture-bound therapies. The problem is that these therapies may not travel well to other cultures. If I, as a therapist, am not willing to understand you, as a client, then I do not value you as a person. This culture clash in therapy (Helman, 1981) is a similar process to culture clash in racism (La Fontaine, 1986), ethnocentrism, the history of oppression, and imperialism. Culture clash exists in sexism, views on sexual orientation, Eurocentrism, Anglocentrism, Americanocentrism, and jingoism. If each culture believes that it alone is supreme, then there is either conflict or an acceptance of a position like that in *Brave New World* (Huxley, 1932).

As finishing remarks, I wish to restate the case for extending Carl Rogers's client-centred therapy. As all counseling inevitably involves the meeting of people from different cultures (Glinga, 1986; Wright-Mills, 1956), backgrounds, and beliefs to ourselves, emphasis needs to be given to the provision of appropriate care for each client and her cultural needs. Counseling and psychotherapy need careful philosophical, ethical, and cultural analyses to identify and acknowledge the presence of culture-bound beliefs (Helman, 1985). Emic psychotherapy research could make a study of the lay beliefs of clients who are suffering socially and psychologically. Such emic research would take care to elucidate modern archetypes of suffering and find the modern mythologies of causation. Western culture-bound disorders that occur rarely or not at all in other countries are such things as obesity, suicide by overdose, anorexia, stress, and agoraphobia. These culture-bound illnesses say a great deal about life in the West. Finally, let us be enriched by meeting with people from diverse cultures, educational backgrounds, and socioeconomic status. Only when we disregard the bonds of our own logic, truth, and life, can we embrace the logics, truths, and lives of others.

References

Douglas, M. (1978). *Cultural bias.* London: Royal Anthropological Institute.

Glinga, W. (1986). Legacy of empire—a journey through British society. Manchester: Manchester University Press.

Grove D.J., & Panzer B. (1989). Resolving traumatic memories—Metaphors and symbols in psychotherapy. New York: Irvington.

Hayley, J. (1973). Uncommon therapy: The psychiatric techniques of Milton Erickson, MD. New York: Norton.

Helman, C.G. (1981). Disease versus illness in general practice. *Journal of the Royal College of General Practitioners, 31,* 548–552.

Helman, C.G. (1985). Psyche, soma and society: The social construction of psychosomatic disorders. *Culture, Medicine and Psychiatry, 9,* 1–26.

Huxley, A. (1932). Brave new world. London: Pam Books.

La Fontaine, J. (1986). Countering racial prejudice: A better starting pint. *Anthropology Today, 2*(6).

Rogers, C.R. (1951). Client centered therapy. Boston: Houghton Mifflin.

Wright-Mills, C. (1956). White collar. New York: Oxford University Press.

An International Model of Counseling: The Authentic Counseling Model

C. Scully Stikes

The objective is to produce a model of counseling that can be adapted by helping professionals in all nations as they work within a pluralistic society. An effective model of counseling that can be adapted by counselors in all nations must deal with cultural universals. The model must be true to the nature and reality of persons throughout the world. Human actions are cultural universals; however, different cultures emphasize different aspects of human actions. In order for a counseling model to be effective, the model must allow for the flexibility of different perspectives on human actions and comprehensively deal with all aspects of human actions.

There are six interrelated components of human actions that are hierarchically related. The first component is *meaning*. Meanings in human actions are values, intents, and imports. These are the reasons why actions occur. There are personal and social meanings in human actions. Second, there are *missions* that are visions, goals, purposes, and directions for which human actions occur. Similarly, there are personal and societal goals and directions. Third, there is *power* in personal and social institutions. Power is the energy by which actions occur. Next, there are *personal and social processes*. These are the activities through which human actions occur, personally and socially. These are the individual coping strategies, formal and informal activities, and the social strategies and formal processes of institutions in society. Then too, there are the *resources* with which actions occur. These are the personalities of individuals and the organizational cultures of institutions. Personalities and organizational cultures are the bases with which personal and institutional actions occur. Last, there are the *sociocultural contexts* in which human actions occur—culture, societies, classes, families—from which all actions are generated. The interaction of these six interrelated components of human action exist in all cultures throughout the world.

The Authenticity Counseling Model

Authenticity in this model refers to the activities, relationships, and structures whose underlying processes are responsive to comprehensive human needs with regard to the diversity of human existence. "A relationship, institution, or society is inauthentic if it gives the appearance of responsiveness which the underlying condition is alienating" (Etzioni, 1968, p. 619). Authenticity requires that the person be conscious, committed, and participate in sharing personal, institutional, and societal power. In order to be authentic in counseling, a counselor must be able to understand the six interrelated components of human action within the framework of the culture of the person being counseled as well as understand the cultural assumptions and values affecting interpersonal relationships. Cultural influences affecting personality, identify formation, and behavior manifestations are generally not part of counseling theories and practices. Counseling approaches have used concepts external to the culture of many clients. The approaches have not used perspectives indigenous to the culture of persons of color or unique elements of their cultures. Furthermore, other barriers to effective counseling have been language differences, class-bound values, and the unstructured process of counseling for persons of color (Atkinson, Morten, & Sue, 1979).

In this model, *life-span development* is composed of developmental tasks and opportunities from infancy to mature adulthood. *Developmental tasks* are those elements that constitute healthy and satisfactory growth in society that individuals must perform. *Opportunities* are the moments the tasks should be achieved (Havighurst, 1967). If the tasks are not achieved at the proper time, they may not be achieved well; they may cause partial or complete failure in other tasks. Tasks can be retraced however difficult they may be. Some tasks result mainly from physical maturation, such as learning to crawl or walk. Other tasks are related to development in society from cultural expectations and pressure, such as social control, personal expression, self-discipline, and peer relations that are a part of the personality of the individual resulting from the interaction of organic and environmental factors.

Operation of the Model

Examining the model from one direction reveals that meanings are the reasons for which human actions occur. Meanings are the initiators of the missions. The missions direct and focus the action and the energies or powers in human action. The use of power moves or modifies personal and social processes and activities. Personal and social powers energize and modify social activities. The person, through activities, structures human actions. Persons behave within the framework of social activities.

From the other perspective, the variables in the model can be limiting or supporting. For instance, if the sociocultural context, the source from which actions occur, is restricted, it ultimately will limit human actions. A restricted society will limit expansion and development. Personal and social resources, when they are not adequate, can limit activities. Without a clear sense of direction, a person has a limited reason for being. An unclear mission distorts the meaning system. Similarly, if each variable is supportive, then the following variables are enriched, expanded, infused, or energized.

The circular and self-modifying system has feedback loops, as described here, that create the authentic human action system that works for individuals and institutions in *any* society. The model provides a framework that is comprehensive and culturally and gender-diverse. It recognizes the flexible and enabling activities for individuals in all cultures and both gender groups. It recognizes the resource base, the impact of personal and social resources on human action. It is a valid system that enhances the elements to meet comprehensive human needs; therefore, it is an authentic system. Understanding and knowing the particular elements of culture, class, clients' family background, gender, personal-social attributes, and stage of life-span development, as well as expressed and diagnosed problems, helping professionals may use the system as a descriptive, explanatory, and diagnostic mechanism to understand, explain, and prescribe certain comprehensive plural actions to develop and to change human functioning over time.

Implications of the Model

Implications of the model are: Helping professionals must play positive roles at every level in developing individuals in the context of any society. The model acknowledges the necessity of various roles for the counselor/therapist as well as others in preventing and resolving human problems. Individuals change in the context of many levels of human functioning—intrapsychic, personality, interpersonal, group, intergroup, social, societal, and cultural. Therefore, long-lived change must encompass plural changes along the multidimensional and multiple levels of human functioning. It is the continual management of changes that is important for individuals to master. The idea is for people to work toward self-efficacy and develop mastery and management of changes in their lives.

There are six essential areas of questions that need to be asked and answered from the helper's and client's perspectives that correspond to each component in the model. One needs to understand their interrelatedness. The answers may vary with individuals and cultures. The questions are:

1. For what reasons do these actions exist?
2. What are the goals and purposes one wishes to achieve?
3. Who is involved (individuals and institutions)? Or what are the energies or driving forces pushing the issues?
4. How are the issues happening? Or how do they operate?
5. What development is needed in personality and what changes are needed in institutional relationships?
6. In what social context does the behavior exist?

Using these questions as diagnostic mechanisms and managing the interacting answers to problems and issues are the keys to maintaining positive health, preventing problems from emerging, and resolving unhealthy issues. The idea is to plan change strategies for each area in the model with the individual as needed. The counselor/therapist must empower the client within the appropriate cultural context. For example, Asian clients may view the counselor as an authority and expect directions to be given; therefore, they may not view the relationship in counseling as symmetrical and expect any sharing of power. However, no one can do anything for clients without their cooperation.

There are a plurality of problems and issues. Therefore, there must be multiple intervention strategies. A problem may touch all dimensions. To be authentic, the questions, intervention strategies, and answers must be personally, socially, and culturally specific.

Furthermore, there must be empathy and *parity* in the relationships in the counseling/therapeutic process whether the relationships are cross-cultural or intercultural. Parity is respect and reciprocal equality in relationships (Lazarus, 1979).

The effective counselor/therapist maintains parity and empathy throughout the therapeutic process. The effective therapist must understand the culture, class, gender, and personal issues of the client, as well as the skills necessary to function in a multicultural environment in order to be effective. Furthermore, the counselor/therapist must understand her- or himself. A counselor needs to know how to effect strategies for the six components relative to self as well as others.

The unit of dynamic analysis for a counselor/therapist is the individual interacting in a group (family, peer, etc.) and the influence of the institutions with which the individual is in contact. It is critically important to look for causes and effects, and interrelationships, not just a single cause or effect. Strategies must involve the search for techniques in all dimensions of human action from the level of the context or existence through resources, activities, the exercise of power or energy, the pursuit of goals, to the search for meaning.

The Outcome of Counseling

The goal of counseling is to create an individual who has mastery over life; who manages human actions for clearly meaningful and definable reasons with a clear direction; who has a sense of personal power and hope for the future; who has control over, and is flexible in managing, his or her relationships and activities; and who is able to influence the acquisition and distribution of adequate resources in a social context.

The end result of counseling or therapy should be producing a person who has a repertoire of coping skills that relate to managing healthy functioning at organic, behavioral, and societal levels. Therefore, dealing with personal and systemic issues is critically important.

A counselor or therapist helps a client to build mastery in managing the changing elements in his or her life at a particular life-span developmental stage and to take advantage of developmental tasks and opportunities as they arise. The individual's life in society is a continuous morphogenic process. The society, institutions, personality, and other factors are all interrelated in the process.

The effective therapist must possess the skills necessary to function in a multicultural environment, must be involved actively with the client, and understand the client's subjective worldview. The counselor/therapist must build rapport, establish a sense of direction, use energy and build hope; find the appropriate etic and emic techniques that work for a particular client; use indigenous support systems effectively; and assist the client to establish mastery.

References

Atkinson, D.R., Morten, G., & Sue, D.W. (1979). *Counseling American minorities: A cross-cultural perspective* (2nd ed.) Dubuque, IA: Wm. C. Brown.

Etzioni, A. (1968). *The active society.* New York: Macmillan.

Havighurst, R.J. (1967). *Developmental tasks in education.* New York: David McKay.

Lazarus, A. (1979, May 11–13). "Multimodal Therapy," Multimodal Therapy Workshop, Multimodal Therapy Institute. Kingston, NJ.

PART II

Economic Issues

One of the most potent of ecologies is that which is economic. Work, jobs, occupations, careers are ways of achieving economic ends but they are ways of achieving psychological, emotional, affiliative, and social ends as well.

But just as there are relationships between the impact of physical ecology on persons of diverse races and cultures, there are also linkages between cultural and racial diversity and access to work, level of work achieved, security of work, and economic development.

The plenary paper that addresses the principal topics of part 2 is presented by Paul Boateng, a member of the British Parliament. A minority group member himself, the Honorable Mr. Boateng earned a law degree from Bristol University, College of Law, and became a solicitor in 1975. He has been extremely active in the cause of human rights and has been a vigorous advocate for improving race relations, inner-city housing, and overseas development. He has effectively utilized churches, community agencies, schools, and private philanthropies to forward the access of ethnic minorities to economic and social opportunities.

Following Mr. Boateng's presentation, three papers address economic issues within the contexts of disability, job displacement, and plateaued workers.

THE ROLE OF COUNSELING IN A MULTIRACIAL, MULTICULTURAL SOCIETY IN AN ECONOMIC CONTEXT

Paul Boateng

It is good to be with you here at Brunel this morning and to share with you some thoughts and concerns about the role of counseling in a multiracial, multicultural society and setting that is within an economic context. I am bound to say also a political one because I do not think that you can easily divide the two types of economic and political settings, as you examine where counseling fits with the needs and concerns of the racial minorities in Britain today. What I want to do is to look at where we have come from as Black people, as Afro-Caribbean and as Asian people, in our society in Britain. I also want to consider where we are going and how counseling touches on that matter.

I think it is important to make it clear from the outset that we as Black people in Britain are not to be seen as simply being newcomers or, indeed, as newcomers at all. All too often, particularly those from overseas, but also those in Britain, somehow believe that until the late 1940s or early 1950s, there were no Black people in Britain. That suddenly out of the blue from the Empire, responding to the call of Mother England to meet the need for relatively cheap supplies of labor in the aftermath of the Second World War, we all jumped off the boat, and prior to that we weren't to be seen. But any examination of British history teaches us otherwise. There have been Blacks in Britain since Roman England. There is evidence of Black Centurians, Black Senators, indeed, and Black Colonial Governors in Britain in the days of the Roman Empire. Coming up more to date, in modern times in the reign of Queen Elizabeth I—modern times, I say, note that—before the United States was effectively settled, the parish records of London show that there were proportionately more Blacks in Elizabethan England than there are Blacks in London today. That is not speculation; that is the parish records and what they show. The situation was such that the Privy Council in the reign of Elizabeth was at one stage exercised with what to do about the situation: the fact that there were so many Blackamoors—as we were then called, around and about in London at that time.

Then, if you go through the history of slavery, you find the importance of Bristol and Liverpool as old established places of Black settlements of freed slaves and of people who were never slaves but who came to Britain to work in the service of the gentlemen and ladies of the time because there was nothing so chic, so fashionable, as to have a little Black boy serving at dinner. If you look at the portraiture of the period, you see Black men and women in that role, but not only in that role. If you look at the history of the theater in the 19th century, there where distinguished Black thespians at work who commanded the stage, and not only in those roles that might naturally fall to them. Such roles went beyond the statutory portrayal of Othello. In terms of the political life of the country, men like Robert Wedderburn and others were found to be the backbone of the radical movement of the 19th century. Many of the social and economic movements of the time saw Black radicals gathering crowds of 15 to 20 thousand in Kennington Gardens—the great center of radical activity and speech.

So, there's that history which is part and parcel of the Black experience in Britain and in London that we are only now beginning to recognize and claim as our own. To be a Black Londoner is not some form of historical aberration. I say that because Blacks in Britain (and it's important to make this distinction at the outset from the situation in the United States), Black Londoners, constantly are faced with the challenge of existing in a society where to be Black and to be British is still regarded by very many people as being something of a contradiction, if not an outright impossibility. That is something an American audience can laugh at, but I can tell you that as far as being Black in Britain is concerned, it is very, very serious because it affects your whole mindset as to where you are, where you belong.

I was born in London although I lived part of my childhood in West Africa. All my children were born in London and, indeed, were born in St. Thomas's hospital. All of them. And yet, all of them, I know, will grow up in a context that somehow denies their Britishness. Thus, that sense of alienation that can all too often lead to bitterness and dislocation within society, is a very real feature of the Black British experience. We still have to win in Britain the argument that it's possible to be Black and British. And for all your Jim Crow legislation and the widespread disadvantage and discrimination that exists in the United States, at least you seem to have overcome that hurdle and you are not only Black Americans when you are winning medals at the Olympic Games. As Blacks in Britain, we always find something slightly ironic about the fact that the only time we ever get the flag draped over us is when we are winning for Britain in the Olympics and, indeed, if they had more of us playing cricket, we would win more often in cricket too.

But there you are. There is a real problem as to where we are now in Britain in terms of a failure to recognize where we are coming from. And, therefore, those engaged in counseling and those who seek to become engaged in counseling within the British context are constantly faced with this problem of identity. Our parents and our grandparents in Britain who come from the African continent, the Caribbean, or the Indian subcontinent, at least have some basis to the proposition that they might at some stage return somewhere else, that there is somehow some sort of home for them elsewhere. But really for my generation and younger, it is an illusion to believe that there is anywhere else. For us come what may, we are here to stay. There is nowhere else and, indeed, there have been instances in which people have thought to return and found the culture shock of going back to the Caribbean, of going back to Africa, of going back to India, something very, very difficult to cope with. Some of these people broke down over there, got stuck over there, or have returned to England and have had to live with a sense of rejection from a place they had considered their own but was not really their own.

I can well remember, and I share it with you bearing in mind that you are an audience of counselors, although it's not something I talk about very much because it is something that caused grave hurt to those who where with me and I don't want them to be identified. But I remember once, when I was much younger, going to a very large international gathering of youth. We had gone one evening to one of the highlights of the event and we had all gone in our different national buses. My friends who were from Jamaica and I became separated from the British bus. They certainly are people who in every sense looked and, indeed, sounded like Jamaicans even though they were born in England or had come to this country when they were very young. We couldn't find the British bus; so they said, all right, come on, we will get on the Jamaican bus, and we did. We were put off the Jamaican bus. Now, I know the hurt they felt as a result of that—the sense of rejection they felt because there they were taking me, who was not Jamaican, onto their bus. I didn't say a word—I might well have been a Jamaican or not—and so I wasn't the reason why they were put off. They were put off because they weren't Jamaican and that really for them was a very, very shattering thing. I ask you to reflect on that in terms of the totality of the experience of that generation of Black youth in Britain. That's the context, it seems to me, within which counselors and counseling too often find themselves in which identity and roots and, therefore, values and self-esteem are a challenge. That's even before we get on to racism, before we get on to the existing pattern of disadvantage and discrimination in our society that is very real.

We have in Britain a situation in which, for the overwhelming majority of Black people, disadvantage and discrimination are major factors of existence and life opportunities in this country. We are set within an urban context because geographically and demographically we are to be found within the city. Set within a context of economic pressure in the sense of a flight of jobs in manufacturing from the inner city and set also within a context of a welfare system that is increasingly crumbling at the edges.

Now, to give you just a brief statistical overview of the situation in Britain today: Over 50 million people in Britain—more than a quarter of the population—are living either under or on the margin of poverty. The number of people on or below supplementary benefit level has gone up by some 55% to 9.4 million since 1979, and the number of children in poverty has almost doubled. So the gap between those who have and those who have not in our society is that much greater than ever before. In terms of the environment in the inner city, you have real disparities of wealth and opportunity in close geographical proximity. If you take an area like Notting Hill or, indeed, Brixton in South London, or my own constituency, you will have areas of public housing in which there is real poverty. This poverty is made worse by the deteriorating environment within the public housing sector in terms of money for rehabilitation and refurbishment of the public housing projects, and increasing overcrowding and pressure because of the lack of new houses built, and because of economic policies that are cutting back on public spending. This country you are visiting, and in which we are living, is a society that is at the heart of the Milton Friedman experiment. You have exported Milton Friedman and his doctrine to us, and you were very wise to export him as quickly as you possibly could because the consequences of living without economic policy are absolutely disastrous. There is a big difference between Thatcher and Reaganite economics. The fact of the matter is that Thatcher actually believes all that Friedman stuff, whereas Reagan never has. That is why you have the massive deficit you have in terms of your public budget. Mrs. Thatcher actually believes it all and she has cut back public spending in every area. So we are living with the consequences of cutting back public spending so far as Black people are concerned.

In the inner city, because some people have done remarkably well over the last 10 years, you find in close geographical proximity housing projects in a state of extreme deterioration and many people within those housing projects experiencing large amounts of and persistent unemployment. I have pockets within my constituency, largely Black pockets, where unemployment is as high as 70% among young people between the ages of 16 and 25—70% unemployed. Within the British context, that is high. I know in the United States that is something you have lived with for many years. One of the frightening things about society is that it is capable of existing with that level of unemployment for certain sectors within it. But that is a new thing so far as Britain is concerned, and it is totally unacceptable. But right next door to such pockets of poverty and employment you will have Georgian terraces; and, four- or five-bedroom detached homes that are selling for a quarter/half a million pounds. That's reality in my own constituency, which has the highest proportion of Black people in the country. You cannot buy a detached four-bedroom house for less than a quarter of a million pounds, which is $400,000 to half a million dollars. You have to understand that is the reality, and next door you have people living in the grip of absolute poverty. Likewise in Notting Hill: beautiful Georgian terraces selling for at least a million pounds for the houses. Next door on the Portabello Estate and almost next door on the Elgin Avenue Estate there is an acute housing crisis. Brixton likewise. Before I became of member of Parliament, my wife and I were living in Brixton. If you said you lived in Brixton, and this was before the uprising there, people thought you were mad. Every upwardly mobile Black professional was seeking to get out of Brixton as fast as possible to Croydon and Merton and those hideous places in the deep south of London. That is where everyone was going. After the uprisings, living in Brixton for everybody, Black and White, began to have some sort of appeal. To buy a flat now on Milton Road, you have to be in a position to pay 55,000 pounds for a one-bedroom flat; a house there, 150,000 pounds. Now that's in Brixton, and yet just down the road there exist continuing deep-rooted disadvantage and discrimination that have not been affected, in my view, one iota by the uprisings in terms of the actual day-to-day experience of living in London for very many Black people.

So you have all this to deal with in terms of how those people who you are seeking to counsel find themselves, with everything reminding them that they are somehow just not up to it. And that must be a feature of your own experience—those of you who counsel in the United States—of the experience of minorities there and, indeed, of poor Whites—when all the messages around you are talking about success, about going places and about wealth and raising up material acquisitions to untold heights, when your own experience is very, very different. And, the ways of going forward in those circumstances are not entirely clear. The opportunities to go forward are themselves limited in terms of attaining jobs, even those jobs with the training scheme that the government currently brings forward. Even given the better jobs within those schemes, recent evidence shows that the employers who participate in those schemes are discriminating against Blacks and doing so quite overtly. So, even on those schemes that pay very little but at least give you access to some form of training, there is the reality of discrimination. In other areas of employment, that is reality, too, and not least in the professional and executive grades. So there is that sense of denial, of rejection, of that low self-image in terms of the way you are ground down by rejection. That, too, is part and parcel of the reality of the Black experience.

Of course, there are lots of escape routes from such rejection: escape routes in terms of descending into a state of apathetic resignation, escape routes in terms of drugs and drink—escape routes not only in terms of a chemically altered state of mind but changes in the state of mind, nevertheless. But there are also escape routes for bright, young entrepreneurs, who ought, if the rhetoric of our society is to be believed, to be finding their way opening up new businesses; they ought to be finding their way economically in a society that is supposed to encourage bright, young entrepreneurs. The reality is, however, that there are two quick ways of acquiring a Porche in our society, both of which, in their different ways, are harmful. The first way is go into the city and to play the markets with a degree of skill and accuracy; in playing around with other people's money, you may acquire a Porche relatively quickly. The other way is to go into drugs, and then in playing around with other people's lives, you may acquire a Porche relatively quickly. Those are the two certain ways of acquiring that much vaunted symbol of success in our society. In our society, the Porche is the ultimate if you are between the ages of 19 and 40 and want to show that you've made it. There are two ways of doing it quickly and I have outlined both of them to you. And that is worrying—that whole mentality, the whole culture that goes with it—has an absolutely devastating effect on the morale, let alone the health of a community. And with the growth of "crack" we are particularly fearful at this time of the impact of crack and crack dealing on the community, not only on the young people who are likely to get involved in the trading and the taking.

But let me give you an example, and it's an example of another factor that I think we have to deal with in terms of looking at where we are today. The extent of the fearfulness that comes from knowing that at the bottom of your block of flats all day and every day, young men are engaged in selling drugs when you, a woman, an elderly man, or indeed, anybody have, in order to get your flat, to go through them. One elderly lady described it to me recently when she came to see me as going through a market of death that she has to go through every morning, every afternoon, whenever she is going to and from her block of flats in Haskell House in Stonebridge. That's the reality. And she has to experience that. So fear and fearfulness are part and parcel, it seems to me, of the reality of counseling today. And then there are those people who, in many ways, are victims of the oppression, of the starvation of resources, of discrimination and disadvantage. But there are also those people who are victims of the reverse of those things who have come through it all, managed to get themselves in a position in which they are achieving, getting places, and who do so through a combination of resolution, resolve, intelligence, hard work, and effort. And, they exist too.

I think it is a great mistake in terms of a multiracial, multicultural society to believe that everybody is failing, everybody is down there and not managing to succeed because *there are those* who are succeeding and who are getting places. But these people are paying a price for that; a price in terms of hyperactivity, constantly being on the go, constantly having to look over their shoulder in order to make sure they are able to preserve what success they have. Many of these people are constantly under pressure from their peers of the same race who are saying, well, the only way she could have got on, she sold out; she must have married a White man; she or he must have done this, that, or the other; otherwise, he or she wouldn't be where they are. It is impossible for a Black man to have done that or to be there unless he sold out. That's the only way. Always a thief or both. So, there's that pressure that comes from within one's own community, and the constant pressure from White colleagues who will always look to you in a situation in which any Black person is involved. If only they were all like you. And even if not said—thought. Now, having to cope with that and all that such experiences bring up inside you. Now that is also, it seems to me, an area where counseling has its role to play. For you are not only counseling in terms of those people who are out there and are not making it and who are under enormous pressure, but you are also counseling those who have made it and are under other types of pressure. In such situations, what it seems counseling has to be about is enabling and empowering those people who are counseled to survive and to endure and to be sustained in their circumstances. Counseling also means helping people to come to grips with their reality and to come to grips with being prepared to change it. It seems to me that counseling has to be a bit more than just reconciling people to their situation. It seems to me that it also has to be about helping them to change it and to empower them. But I look to you to guide me on that and to take that issue forward. In my view, you cannot deal with this issue unless you are trained to deal with it. Instinct alone, sympathy alone, is not enough, it seems to me. There has to be a recognition of the historical background; there has to be a recognition of where the linguistic and cultural factors are relevant that go to make up effective counseling in a multiracial and multicultural society so we don't misread the signals that are sent out and we don't miss the messages that come forward.

That, it seems to me, is the context in which we examine this issue. In terms of where we are going I have to tell you that Black folks are very, very good at surviving; we've survived 400 years of what has been dished out to us by the world in which we find ourselves. But I see now in the communities, as far as Britain is concerned, more than survival on the agenda. I think you find in Britain today a much more self-confident Black community than you found before. You find more Black people who are determined to come together as Blacks but also to come together in alliance with the wider community in order to change the conditions in which we live and to have a degree of self-confidence as professionals and as workers within community organizations and community groups that did not exist a decade ago. I find, in terms of my daily life, a determination to do that and to go forward, a much higher public profile for good and ill, a determination to win and to overcome the difficulties that face us. And despite all those difficulties, as a community I feel more optimistic about Black people and about our multiracial society now that I did 10 years ago.

But the context is still one that we have to change because of that conflict between being Black and British. The context is still, for all too many of our people, one of constant deprivation and disadvantage. The context is still one of danger for all too many in their experiences on housing estates and in communities where attacks or racial harassment are an everyday feature of life when going shopping, going to school, or when parents come and pick children up from school. That too is part and parcel of the reality. But if you ask me about the future, I say we go beyond survival to success and we look to professional organizations and professionals like yourselves to be with us on that march. One thing has to be said. Although the race dimension is important and we are all influenced and affected by that, if you look at the great themes of our world, race and racial equality is one of them. But racial equality can never be separated from that wider struggle for social and economic justice. So when we engage on this issue of how we respond in a multicultural/multiracial society, how we make a success of that society, we also engage on the issue of how we make a success of our society full stop, how we make a success of living together, whether we are Black or White, whether we are Afro, Caribbean, Asian, Hispanic, Anglo, wherever we come from. Because if we can't address effectively the issue of race within the context of social and economic justice, we are never going to be able to address those social and economic justice issues at all properly, and we are never going to be able to build a society that is stable, peaceful, that allows us all to grow and to maximize our potential as human beings. At the end of the day that's what counseling certainly is about, and I believe that politics ought to be about that too. Thank you very much.

ECONOMIC ISSUES WORKSHOPS

Part 2 concludes with three papers from the workshops at Brunel University that address economic issues in ecological contexts of both British and American origin. Each of these papers addresses the counseling of a population that is characterized by a negative economic ecology. For example, Roma Drevets proposes a conceptual model concerned with counseling those who have experienced job displacement that focuses on the self, the learning or relearning of skills for daily living, and the development of possibilities for the future. William J. Stewart and Charles J. VanderKolk's paper addresses the unique needs for counseling and the approaches likely to be useful in dealing with minorities with disabilities who experience unemployment and underemployment. Finally, David Whitfield deals with counseling plateaued workers, those whose ecological context is characterized as one in which the likelihood of additional hierarchical promotion is very low.

These papers, individually and collectively, argue from different perspectives that, as Paul Boateng has eloquently argued in his plenary paper, counselors need to help empower people to change their circumstances. To do so, however, frequently requires one to reaffirm the self and to rediscover one's personal worth as a platform from which to launch into new and comprehensive economic possibilities.

Change: A Blessing or a Curse?

Roma Drevets

With jobs and occupations, we are not constant, we change with the times. It is our attitudes and willingness to meet these changes as ladders rather than stumbling stones, and as opportunities rather than defeats, challenges, and obstacles that allow us to achieve despite change.

The problem of job displacement poses numerous challenges for the client and the counselor. Not only must the counselor deal with the problems of reprogramming the worker, but also with the worker's own loss and feelings of worthlessness. The focus of this paper is primarily on the role of the counselor in working with these individuals. To successfully attain such goals, the counselor must acquire a basic understanding of, and an enhanced philosophical approach to, preventing serious depression, disruptive behavior, and permanent unemployment.

Barton (1983) emphasized the importance of a positive attitude in working with these clients. In addition, Evans (1979) warned of the possibility of professionals being forced to join the dislocated worker ranks. And Jones (1979), in working with these individuals, reminded us of the trauma these workers experience. At the same time, Hurst and Shepard (1985) related the resistance workers undoubtedly display in regard to relocating.

We know that the nature of work is changing rapidly due to many factors, and counselor needs to be aware of their local ramifications. For example, the U.S. census estimates that the work force in the United States will increase only by 10% by the year 2000; but in Asia and the Pacific it will increase 55% and in Latin America and Africa by 80% (Naisbitt, 1982). In addition, Toffler (1980) in *The Third Wave,* proposed that whereas workers in the past were often rewarded for plodding bureaucratic behavior and blind obedience, the workers of the future will be rewarded for accepting responsibility, being able to deal with rapid change, accepting ever more complex tasks, and being sensitively tuned to the people around them.

Literature in the field of career development has not placed enough emphasis on rebuilding the self before relocating the person. As one deals with developing or restructuring the inner self, it is also important to work on improving social skills. Group counseling offers an excellent framework for recognizing that all human beings have spiritual selves. I propose a new direction for training and research. Building on work in inner strength and development, I advocate a conceptual model that provides an integrative framework for understanding the role of work in structuring self.

Barton (1983) reminded us that it is vital to have a positive attitude toward dislocated clients. He further related that their jobs have gone for good, that their skills are obsolete, but that there is hope for a new future. Evans (1979) felt that in the next century, professionals, too, will be swelling the ranks of the unemployed. The vulnerability of the professions, he said, is that they act as the exclusive repositories and disseminators of specialist knowledge. Increasingly, this knowledge will be made available to the layman by computer. Change is constant and we are always becoming. Therefore, the philosophy and outlook of the counselor and the client must be one that welcomes change.

Involuntary careers loss generally is a sudden and traumatic (perhaps devastating) change for an individual (Jones, 1979). Before a client can begin to consider the idea of a new job, he or she must work with the loss of the old one. The necessity of identifying and beginning a new career, when the needs for security, self-direction, purpose, and future are not being fulfilled, results in turmoil. The client grieves the loss of a job as much or more that the loss of other personal possessions. This grieving accentuates the turmoil. It is important here for the client to experience a healing process. A counselor's understanding of this is critical in the effective assistance of individuals who are experiencing such a crisis.

Human beings grieve as a result of significant loss and because their life has been diminished in some aspect. Individuals must deal with this. However, the counselor must help clients to realize that each chance, each feeling, each responsibility they commit themselves to adds richness to their inner strength.

Counseling dislocated workers requires some understanding of and appreciation for the unique effects of unemployment on individuals. Jones (1979) identified three grief stages that such workers experience: (1) numbness after notification of the event; (2) yearning and protest characterized by insomnia, loss of appetite, and other physiological reactions often accompanied by anger; and (3) apathy, aimlessness, and disorganization characterized by a disinclination to look toward the future or to see any purpose in life. The first step for a counselor is to listen without judging the client. It is essential to validate clients as people and as workers, and to accept their feelings about their job loss and search. One important aspect of counseling unemployed workers is to help them make a clear distinction between their lack of control over the economy and their total control and responsibility for their subsequent job search, emotional responses, and future lives.

Simply giving the individual permission to grieve is often helpful. Encouraged to make contact with the full extent of feelings and thoughts resulting from the loss can be of significant help to a client. If the grief can be naturally experienced and worked through immediately following the career loss, it is much less likely to create problems later (Jones, 1979).

Through counseling dislocated workers, Hurst and Shepard (1985) found that the typical dislocated worker tended to resist career assessment, vocational guidance or counseling, job-search training, and personal support. Identifying this resistance and confronting the clients with it was a major challenge. Many clients merely wanted their old jobs back or were only interested in job referrals. Many workers hoped they would be recalled by their former employers; this hope prevented them from conducting a fully committed search for a new job. Many were so emotionally enmeshed in regaining their benefits and going back to their prior jobs that they resisted considering other possibilities.

Besides dealing with this aspect, the counselor must encourage the learning or relearning of skills for daily living that enable a person to function effectively in a changing society. Dislocated clients often have negative attitudes and feelings about employment agencies. They are frequently skeptical and suspicious. Feeling degraded, ignored, angry, frustrated, and hopeless, they generally consider training as a waste of time (Hurst & Shepard, 1985). Many set a personal "minimum wage" and will not work for less.

Work taps the spiritual world and supplies strength and growth. Rose (1981) stated in his article that, through work, one can feel God-like. Counselors must acknowledge the spiritual aspect of work in counseling. To succeed in helping the client deal with his or her temporary displacement, the counselor must be creative.

I have discussed thus far in this paper one aspect that I feel the counselor must be prepared to work with in helping dislocated persons. However, to perform an adequate counseling task, it would be necessary to have a counseling center for such persons. At this center, all pertinent areas would be covered by workshops, group counseling sessions, and individual sessions. Ideally, these areas would cover the following aspects: the spiritual, the cultural, the intellectual, the moral, the physical, the social, and finally, the economic.

To most people, nothing is more important than being successful. That is why it is crucial in working with dislocated persons that all areas of the self be developed. Success breeds success, and failure breeds failure. Above all, a counseling center working with dislocated persons mus imbed in their clients the ability to look forward to change, to the new person he or she is becoming. The client will have the wisdom that the present self lacks. He or she will have learned to live life more fully and will have acquired, through experience, a perspective that lends peace to all situations. We must learn to trust the gift of change. Change: A blessing or a curse? The choice still remains an individual one.

Bibliography

Barton, P.E. (1983). Retooling the work force. *Vocational Education, 58,* 22–24.
Evans, C. (1979). *The micro millennium.* New York: Viking.
Hurst, J.B., & Shepard, J.W. (1985). Counseling dislocated workers in job training placement act title III programs. *The Vocational Guidance Quarterly, 34,* 47–52.
Jones, W.H. (1979). Grief and involuntary career change: Its implications for counseling. *The Vocational Guidance Quarterly, 27,* 196–201.
Naisbitt, J. (1982). *Megatrends.* New York: Warner.
Rose, M. (1981) The feel of a writer's work: An inquiry into the phenomenology of work. *Vocational Guidance Quarterly, 29,* 236–243.
Toffler, A. (1980). *The third wave.* New York: Morrow.

Counseling in Relation to Unemployment and Underemployment of Minorities With Disabilities

William J. Stewart and Charles J. VanderKolk

Individuals with disabilities are almost always more likely to have to face and deal with problems of unemployment and underemployment than the nondisabled (Geist & Calzaretta, 1982). Although the proportion of young non-White minority group members earning the high school diploma is approaching that of Whites, non-White high school graduates aged 18 to 24 in 1986 experienced 2 ½ times the risk of unemployment of all high school graduates in that age group (Bureau of Labor Statistics, 1983).

Minorities with disabilities face an even bleaker employment outlook (Wright, 1988). Minorities with disabilities in the United States have been described as having a higher rate of unemployment and underemployment, a lower educational achievement level, a lower income level, a higher rate of disabling conditions, and a higher potential of becoming disabled. Unfortunately, researchers project that the future of these Americans, who have been numbering up to 50 million, is likely to repeat the past (Bowe, 1985; National Council on the Handicapped, 1988).

According to the Hudson Institute (Semerad, 1987), key employment trends that will shape the last years of the 20th century include the slow growth and aging of the work force, the feminization of the work force, and a proportional increase of minorities and minorities with disabilities, along with a 32% decrease in the number of native White men entering the work force through the year 2000. New jobs in service industries are expected to demand much higher skill levels than the jobs of today, resulting in greater joblessness among the least skilled and educationally disadvantaged. Accordingly, professionals and policymakers working with these individuals must be aware of these trends and must commit themselves in several ways. What will be needed is improvement in the educational preparation of all workers; the full integration of minority workers, including Black and Hispanic workers, into the economy; resolution/reconciliation of the conflicting needs of women, work, and families; the maintenance of the dynamism of an aging work force; and the full utilization of the talents of disabled individuals. These needs must be met if the American labor force is to adapt to the rapidly changing nature of the workplace to compete in a global economy and to meet the goal of full employment. To the extent that other countries experience similar problems with their citizens who are minorities or disabled, these recommendations would apply to their economies.

Significant Problems of Minorities With Disabilities

In many ways methods for counseling minorities with disabilities are similar to those used to counsel any person with problems or with decisions to be made. Yet, there are particular problems and situations that have a greater impact upon this population, and the following points should be considered:

1. Career development may have been rather unsystematic and influenced more by chance because of a lack of opportunity or exposure to normal personal, social, and vocational experiences.

2. The disability itself often affects access to the labor market. The disabled person may also be unwilling to move away from family, friends, and familiar places.

3. Cultural-ethnic barriers to placement exist and include language or language difficulties, and moral-religious barriers that prohibit the individual from being willing to work on a certain day, perform a particular job, or be in a particular work setting.

4. Litigation may be involved, and the individual could be seeking compensation for on-the-job injuries from the employer through worker's compensation or may be seeking Social Security disability or other benefits.

5. The family situation may be a tremendous factor to be considered; for example, the single family homemaker who is disabled and is faced with being the primary caretaker of children and having to earn a living at the same time.

6. The disincentives that exist when wages earned do not exceed welfare or disability benefits for the disabled individual and other family members.

7. Diminished self-esteem, limited interpersonal skills, and lack of "motivation" often become predominant because of a broader society that tends to devalue differences—such as belonging to a minority racial and ethnic group with differing beliefs, customs and values—as do emotional/mental, physical, economic, or educational limitations, all of which carry stereotypical perceptions of difference that have a stigmatizing effect.

8. The higher incidence of alcoholism and drug addiction than in the general population is a major social, personal, and economic problem.

9. The educational and training levels are lower than for Whites.

10. Minorities with disabilities are less likely to be provided education or training, are more likely to be screened out; but, if found eligible for vocational rehabilitation services, are less likely to be rehabilitated.

11. They have to perform heavier, more physically demanding work than do Whites, resulting in more or additional injuries.

Counseling Strategies Needed to Ensure Personal, Social, and Vocational Success for Minorities With Disabilities

The diversity of variables and considerations identified in this paper underscores the critical need for counseling and rehabilitation professionals to recognize and better understand the dynamic and complex nature of the needs of minorities with disabilities, and to serve as advocates for them from identification and initial referral, through successful job placement and follow-up. It seems critical that the counseling professional gather all relevant, credible information useful to the counseling of minorities with disabilities who are unemployed or underemployed.

In the process of developing this paper, we uncovered several ways the counseling and rehabilitation professional can better serve this population. Among the recommendation for counselor are:

1. Gain information and knowledge of minority beliefs, values, life-styles, economic conditions, vocational development, cultures, and the interrelationship of these factors.
2. Develop a habit of assessing and evaluating the needs and potentials of individual clients with the clients themselves; do this on an ongoing basis throughout involvement with each case; and document this assessment and evaluation in an individualized counseling plan.
3. When provision of actual counseling or rehabilitation service has begun, begin providing regular and frequent follow-up services in order to prevent premature termination of services, to document progress, and to ensure that services provided are appropriate, timely, and effective.
4. When possible, include family members and significant others in the counseling process and do this on a regular basis.
5. When beginning the job-placement counseling phase of the client's plan, be sure to be up to date on the labor market, individual employers, and how individual jobs might be modified to accommodate the individual with the disability.
6. After job placement make sure that periodic follow-up services are provided for a long enough time to ensure that the client and employer can work through any problems and frustrations.

It is also recommended that counseling professionals be totally aware of community resources that could provide support for the client during and after counseling services; and that they facilitate the identification of potential training needs and service delivery issues by reviewing existing training and service delivery programs, identifying research needs, and developing alternative service patterns. In addition, counseling professionals need to begin or continue to educate potential employers about the special needs and characteristics of minorities with disabilities, through work with such programs as projects with industry, employee assistance programs, and employee intervention programs. Finally, counseling professionals should serve as advocates for the establishment of preservice and in-service training of counselors that will enhance their ability to provide appropriate services and establish minority advisory groups to enhance the habilitation or rehabilitation of minorities with disabilities through provision of more effective services as well as policy and funding influence.

In summary, if the determination of needs, appropriate treatment strategies, extent of vocational disability, and planning for enhanced work and personal adjustment are to be meaningful and beneficial for minorities with disabilities, acknowledgment of the kinds of characteristics identified throughout this paper seems critical. If the psychosocial and vocational lives of this population of disabled persons are to be maximized through the provision of appropriate counseling services, each individual client must be better understood.

References

Bowe, F. (1985). *Disabled adults in America.* Washington, DC: U.S. Government Printing Office.

Bureau of Labor Statistics, U.S. Department of Labor. (1983, July 28). Working mothers. Reported in *USA Today*, p. 1.

Geist, C.S., & Calzaretta, W.A. (1982). *Placement handbook for counseling disabled persons.* Springfield, IL: Charles C Thomas.

Wright, T.J. (1988). Enhancing the professional preparation of rehabilitation counselors for improved services to ethnic minorities with disabilities. *The Journal of Applied Rehabilitation Counseling, 19*(4), 4–10.

Understanding and Counseling the Plateaued

David Whitfield

Organizations are just as multicultured as societies; thus, counseling procedures that work in one organizational setting may totally fail in another, especially when it comes to counseling the plateaued. Plateauing is one of the most serious nemeses for managers in corporations today. An understanding of the magnitude, forms, and symptoms of plateauing will help counseling professionals to be better prepared to render effective assistance to the plateaued person.

This paper defines plateauing, addresses its magnitude, forms, and symptoms, and suggests ways that traditionally educated and trained counselors may prepare themselves to help the numerous plateaued managers.

Plateauing

First, what is plateauing and some of its various definitions? Conceptually, a plateau has been defined as a point in one's career at which the likelihood of additional hierarchical promotion is very low (Veiga, 1981). Plateauing, per Bardwick (1986), is a natural phenomenon that occurs in its various forms in all phases of our lives. Warren, Ference, and Stoner (1975) further gave a clearer definition as it directly affects managers. Specifically, it means that there is little or no chance that managers will be promoted or receive substantial increases in duties and responsibilities. It also implies being in a job for a long time, and perceiving that few chances for advancement exist in the organization (Hartman & Perlman, 1984). As counselors can see, the definition of plateauing is relatively fluid, but the magnitude is clear.

The Magnitude of Plateauing

Throughout their careers, most managers spend the last 10 to 20 years plateaued (Lorsch & Takagi, 1986). An example these authors give is that 80% to 90% of the managers at IBM are long-term employees and most are plateaued, and that of General Electric's 83,000 managers and professionals, more than 50% are plateaued and have been for many years. Their study also points out that at Bethlehem Steel, 80% of its managers are career managers and most of them are plateaued.

However, Veiga (1981) conducted a survey with three corporations each employing over 100,000 people. He selected 1,733 managers up to and including the vice president. Veiga suggested that the number of plateaued managers is less than 50%. Managers were classified as plateaued if tenure in their present position was equal to or greater than 7 years. The tenure in those plateaued in their present position ranged from 7 to 30 years; their ages ranged from 40 to 64 years. Veiga looked at six positions, specifically, to determine at which of the six positions plateauing begins. He found that plateauing begins as early as the third position, where stay time increases significantly. This means that these managers are being increasingly passed over for promotion, that they are organizationally or structurally plateaued. Plateauing is not only inevitable but it also is taking place more rapidly and markedly than in the past (Warren et al., 1975). Thus one may infer that the number of plateaued managers is increasing relatively fast. If counselors look at the number of corporations in America, they may conclude with certainty that the size of the plateaued population is large, which implies that there are many opportunities for the properly trained counselor.

The Forms of Plateauing

The counselor can gain a needed perspective on what helping approach to take to assist the plateaued person by knowing the three forms that plateauing takes: (a) structural, (b) content, and (c) life plateauing (Bardwick, 1986).

Structural plateauing is more readily apparent than the other two. Because organizations are hierarchical or pyramidal, the higher the corporate rungs, the lower the probability is of getting to the top rung. And as the pyramid gets higher, the number of slots or positions decreases significantly, and so does the opportunity to move upward.

The top of the pyramid is expanding much more slowly than is the middle (Warren, Ference, & Stoner, 1975), and managers who advanced rapidly during the 1960s are now just below the top. Structural plateauing (Bardwick, 1986) refers to the end of promotions. However, this is not new, but what is new and troubling is that people will be structurally plateaued at an increasing rate, which means they will be plateaued earlier than they anticipated. Thus, they will remain there and perhaps overlearn their jobs.

When people know their jobs too well they are **content plateaued** because there is little or nothing new to learn. People need a challenge—challenge means learning and the absence of it necessarily leads to boredom. Whereas in large organizations structural plateauing is inescapable, content plateauing is not. According to Bardwick, large organizations provide more opportunities to move laterally for new and challenging work than do small organizations. On the other hand, in small organizations, content plateauing is a constant concern for managers because there are fewer opportunities for lateral movement. This form of plateauing is preventable and remediable (Bardwick, 1986).

Though Bardwick points out that large organizations provide lateral movement to prevent plateauing, this writer experienced plateauing in an extremely large organization that had thousands of lateral possibilities; yet many people get locked into a specific occupational group or career pattern and it is extremely difficult for them to move out of a rigidly prescribed path. However, this writer's experience supports Bardwick's notion that once plateaued, a person experiences depression, a lost of self-esteem, a lack of motivation, the inability to concentrate, stress, bitterness, an "I don't care" attitude, and many other psychological variables familiar to counselors. What is most disconcerting is that there is no one to talk to and everything becomes bottled up inside. Being plateaued is shattering to self-esteem, especially if work is the main focus of one's life, which leads to plateauing in life.

Plateauing in life is inevitable when work becomes the most crucial part of one's life, as Bardwick states. Work may be the sole source of self-esteem, as long as managers are growing and being promoted. When promotions inevitably end, managers feel an acute sense of failure. Though the understanding of these three forms of plateauing is crucial for counseling, it is also important to be sensitive to the behaviors of plateaued persons.

A study conducted by Hartman and Perlman (1984) involved managers from 109 mental health agencies. The study identified four groups of managers and some of their behaviors. The four groups were: (1) those psychologically and organizationally plateaued; (2) those psychologically plateaued but not organizationally identified as plateaued; (3) those organizationally identified as plateaued but not psychologically plateaued; and (4) those neither psychologically nor organizationally plateaued. The results showed that psychologically plateaued managers were not only alienated from their work but also from the community. These managers were found to be more sensitive than their non-plateaued counterparts to role variables. Specifically, they had significantly lower identification with the organization and were less satisfied with both intrinsic and extrinsic job factors.

The Symptoms of Plateauing

For many managers plateauing in organizations is as inevitable as death, and the symptoms are varied and numerous. They are subsumed under four categories (Bardwick, 1986): passiveness, work symptoms, general symptoms, and busyness. Without boring the reader with long lists, a few symptoms from each category are offered.

The plateaued manager, when passive, manifests the "I don't care" attitude about work, noninvolvement, a lack of initiative, a lack of energy, a lack of specific goals, the inability to make decisions, and withdrawal from others. Descriptive of work symptoms are: due dates are missed, work needs redoing, incomplete work, work being put off, no sense of urgency, and work is not getting done.

The third category is general symptoms, where the plateaued manager experiences an increase in illness, being overly critical of others, not helping others, tenseness or irritability, with a tendency to fly off the handle, an increase in the use of drugs, alcohol, and tobacco, and frequent depression. The symptoms of the last category, busyness, are: working very long hours but not productively or creatively, and complaining of being too busy at home to complaining of being too busy to have time for self. Whereas this writer lists only a few symptoms, Bardwick listed 57 known symptoms of the plateaued person. Adding the age variable to plateauing makes the counselor's job more challenging because in many instances the plateaued manager is an older person. Do the counseling professionals have the education and training necessary to render assistance effectively to this plateaued age group? Gross (1988) suggested that most practicing counselors have had little or no experience or training in working with older persons. So the helping equation becomes quite complex when we add age to an already challenging population to counsel.

Counseling the Plateaued

The corporate setting is a promising area for the counseling profession. According to Bardwick, managers will not counsel. Not only will they not do it, but most cannot. Most managers do not know how to handle emotional encounters (Bardwick, 1986). Bardwick further points out that that managers don't have the counseling tools or the behavior necessary to assist a plateaued person. Most managers don't want to counsel. This, given the size of the plateaued population, is a fruitful area for the properly trained counselor.

Because the corporate setting is newer than the clinical setting to most counselors, it is more appropriate to address the corporate setting. Traditionally trained counselors if they are to provide assistance in the corporate setting, may require retooling (Smith, 1988).

Retooling may be necessary because (a) traditionally trained and educated counselors are ill equipped to render effective services in the corporate setting, as Smith says; (b) strategies for counseling those who are underemployed (plateaued) are not well developed (Hesketh, Shouksmith, & Kang, 1987); and (c) organizations have different cultures.

Schein (1987) pointed out that counselors cannot function effectively unless they know a good deal about the culture in which they are working. Thus, counselors who render services to the plateaued in an organizational setting must understand that organization's culture. Schein further stated that "...it is crucial to understand as much as possible about the culture within which one is operating so that one can capitalize on that understanding in trying to be helpful" (Schein, p. 78).

Counselors are already familiar with what culture means in a general sense. However, in organizations, culture is defined in a slightly different context. Culture is the acquired knowledge that people use to interpret experience and generate social behavior (Luthans, 1985). Luthans added that this view of culture emphasizes both *content and meaning*, and is most applicable to organizational behavior. Organizational culture (Gibson, Ivancevich, & Donnelly, 1988) means a system of values, beliefs, and norms that organizational members share. Culture used in this context has variables that a counselor should understand in order to be more effective.

The variables are subsumed under managerial functions and organizational characteristics (Gibson et al., 1988). Under managerial functions the variables are: (a) planning, (b) organizing, (c) leading, and (d) controlling. Under organizational characteristics they are: (a) behavior, (b) structure and process. Though organizations are multicultured, a thorough understanding of decision counseling (Janis & Mann, 1977) will make counseling in organizations highly accepted and acted upon. By applying decision counseling properly, the counselor can foster a relationship that is socially rewarding and professionally fruitful for the plateaued manager. In this procedural intervention, Janis and Mann suggested a set of diagnostic questions (see Janis & Mann, chapter 14) to be answered by the counselor for him- or herself; answering these questions will improve the counselor's vigilant problem-solving skills, especially in the corporate setting.

Counselors can make themselves more viable by understanding organizational culture and by: (a) learning management terminology (Smith, 1988), reading corporate literature and taking business courses, and (b) researching such journals as: *Training and Development Journal, Personnel Administration, Training Journal, Personnel, EAP Digest,* and *Organizational Dynamics.*

Egan (1986) suggested another consideration to increase counselor effectiveness in this setting: the Problem-Management Model. This model is a cognitive-behavioral approach to counseling and psychotherapy. It takes advantage of the vast amount of research that has been done on the problem-solving process itself, which focuses on human problem solving. The counseling skills necessary in applying this model, according to Egan, include establishing: (a) working relationships; (b) basic and advanced communications skills; (c) challenges where clients (the plateaued) can help themselves; (d) problem clarification; (e) goal setting; (f) program development and program implementation; and (g) ongoing evaluation.

Additionally, this writer suggests that by attending management seminars, doing case studies and analyses of those cases, taking a course in organizational behavior, and studying the social psychology of organizations and the instruments that pertain to organizational behavior, counselors will become more skillful in helping the plateaued in the organizational setting.

Most of the literature reviewed by this writer indicates that traditionally trained and educated counselors are not adequately prepared to help the plateaued. However, counselors *are* best equipped to deal with this nemesis because they have the foundation and they can: (a) help emphasize the plateaued person's choices; (b) listen without the superiority baggage; (c) be empathic, sensitive listeners; (d) deal effectively with emotional responses; (e) help the plateaued without the managerial judgmental factor; (f) help the plateaued see that perhaps this is a stage in life where change is exigent; (g) help him or her to see opportunities for growth; (h) help the plateaued see the situation as an opportunity for growth rather than a sign or failure; (i) help the plateaued see that this is a mid-life crisis that is an extreme case of the normal process of mid-life transition (Davis & Gould, 1981); that transitions are "critical" decision periods between progress and stagnation; and (j) help the plateaued person address such questions as: (a) What are my options? (b) What do I do next? (c) Where am I now? (d) Where do I want to go? and (e) How do I get there?

Summary

The corporate sector is another area for the counseling professional to excel, but a clear understanding of both the plateaued and the corporate cultures is essential. With a clear understanding of plateauing, its symptoms, and the plateaued person, plus an understanding of organizational culture, the counselor will be more solidly prepared to render effective help to members of this large population. This may help the United States regain its competitive edge. However, as Smith (1988) pointed out, counselors' move from education to business and other settings (cultures) is often difficult and frustrating. When counselors are prepared to help the plateaued, an essential question to answer is: Which counseling procedures hold the best promise for the plateaued?

References

Bardwick, J.M. (1986). *The plateauing trap*. New York: American Management Association.

Davis, S.M., & Gould, R.L. (1981, July-August). Three vice presidents in mid-life. *Harvard Business Review,* pp. 118–130.

Egan, G. (1986). *The skilled helper.* Belmont, CA: Brooks/Cole.

Gibson, J.L., Ivancevich, J.M., & Donnelly, J.H., Jr. (1988). *ORGANIZATIONS, Behavior structure, processes.* Plano, TX: Business Publications.

Gross, D.R. (1988). Counseling the elderly: Strategies, procedures, and recommendations. *Counseling and Human Development, 21*(4).

Hartman, A.E., & Perlman, B. (1984, August). *Career plateaus of public sector managers.* Paper presented at the Annual Convention of the American Psychological Association (92nd), Toronto, Ontario, Canada.

Hesketh, B., Shouksmith, G., & Kang, J. (1987). A case study and balance sheet approach to unemployment. *Journal of Counseling and Development, 66,* 175–179.

Janis, I.L., & Mann, L. (1977). *Decision making, A psychological analysis of conflict, choice and commitment.* New York: Free Press.

Lorsch, J.W., & Takagi, H. (1986, July-August). Keeping managers off the shelf. *Harvard Business Review,* pp. 60–65.

Luthans, F. (1985). *Organizational behavior* (4th ed.). New York: McGraw Hill.

Schein, E.H. (1987). *Process consultation, lessons for managers and consultants.* Reading, MA: Addison-Wesley.

Smith, R.L. (1988). Counseling and human resource development: Response to "career development in business and industry." *Journal of Counseling and Development, 66,* 382–384.

Veiga, J.F. (1981). Plateaued versus nonplateaued managers: Career patterns, attitudes, and path potential. *Academy of Management Journal, 24,*(3) 566–578.

Warren, K.E., Ference, T.P., & Stoner, J.A.F. (1975, January-February). Case of the plateaued performer. *Harvard Business Review,* pp. 30–38, 147–148.

PART III

Social Issues

Although each of the ecological emphases discussed in the four parts of this monograph are important and interactive, each has a different contribution to the whole. Social issues have to do with living in community with others. The negative side of such an ecology has to do with the barriers—including racism and prejudice—that separate culturally different groups from each other and that preclude members of each group from trusting and communicating effectively with members of other groups.

In the outline of the plenary paper addressed to part 3, social issues, Dr. Omar Daniels, senior consulting psychiatrist at Princess Alexandra Hospital, the United Kingdom, speaks specifically to the degree to which approaches to therapy are sensitive to cultural diversity, how racial and cultural factors influence mental health, and how counselors can address clients' themes within their therapeutic approach. Such issues play at the base of cross-cultural counseling. They need to be placed within a frame of reference that acknowledges how social factors affect the stress, insecurity, behavioral problems, attitudes, and psychiatric disorders that different immigrant and minority groups experience.

Following Dr. Daniels's presentation, several papers address counselor roles in promoting intercultural understanding, combating racism and cultural bias, and reducing the stereotypes associated with the White counselor-Black client interaction.

SOCIAL ISSUES OF COUNSELING FOR CULTURAL AND RACIAL DIVERSITY IN BRITAIN AND THE UNITED STATES

Omar Daniels

Sociocultural Perspective on Therapy

Therapy, when used in the broadest sense, is not unique to the West, and its variants are seen in many diverse cultures and societies. The forms of therapy are as varied as the different concepts of illness and definitions of "need" and reflect different societies. The development and evolution of therapy and counseling in the West have been the most well documented. Psychotherapy can be seen as ultimately deriving from a central body of theory. This theory has enriched our understanding of developmental, familial, and interpersonal processes, but it is firmly rooted in the values and culture of Western Europe. These values are themselves commendable—for example, the possibility of individual change; the belief that developmental influences determine the adult personality; the belief that personality deficits can be corrected by learning.

In connection with these therapeutic assumptions are concepts of a homogeneous population and universal psychological and developmental processes. Contrasting with these ideas is evidence that access to psychotherapy is certainly not universal and various groups are excluded. Minority groups have begun to question the relevance of broadly based approaches to their needs.

Therapies have always existed in a political context and have been barometers of societal processes. In addition, the social significance of therapy includes the question of whether it moves people in progressive or constructive directions or produces stagnation and conformity. These issues might be explored most effectively by looking at "common unhappiness" in the context of cultural and racial diversity of the U.K.

Racial and Cultural Factors in Mental Health in the U.K.

When analyzing various racial and cultural factors influencing mental health in the United Kingdom, one is compelled to consider examination of the following:

- Developmental factors such as self-concept and social identity;
- Sociopolitical factors such as issues related to the immigration processes and specific problems of minority groups like racial harassment; and
- Psychological factors including the mental aspects of stress, insecurity, behavioral problems, antisocial attitudes and behavior, and psychiatric illness or breakdown.

An analysis of these factors specific to the U.K. minority group experience with reference to mental health can provide the background for a framework in which cross-cultural therapy can be practiced.

Sociopolitical Context of Therapy in the U.K.

The theory exists that historical and political circumstances in the United Kingdom produce a level of objective reality that should determine and direct one's orientation, bias, and training in counselling and therapy. In connection with a cross-cultural sphere, specific problems germane to ethnic minorities in terms of mental health care can be categorized generally as educational, psychological, occupational, linguistic, legal, and racial.

Summary

Transcultural counseling embraces racial and cultural factors that affect therapy. Such factors, which need to be taken into consideration, include the integration of national concepts with global approaches, development of positive and appropriate attitudes, and formation of culturally sensitive service delivery models and research. These models require sociocultural components of a global village embodying children in the streets of places such as Beijing, Iran, South Africa, Colombia, and Germany. Clients' themes should be included in the counselors' therapeutic approaches, for in doing so, the client adds meaning to counselors' meaning.

SOCIAL ISSUES WORKSHOPS

Part 3 concludes with four workshop papers that address social issues from different vantage points. Professor Larry C. Loesch, University of Florida, discusses counselor roles that can help alleviate the stresses that cultural minorities experience in intercultural adoption. Such roles include the counselor as promoter of intercultural understanding, the counselor as counselor, the counselor as resource consultant, and the counselor as reality marker.

In the second paper, Professors Donelda A. Cook and Janet E. Helms, University of Maryland, discuss the role of counselors in combating the "new racism" at predominantly White universities. The paper focuses on the overt and covert bases of racism in higher education as well as counselor intervention at the institutional level and with individual students.

The third paper, by Robert Jacque Chapman, visiting assistant professor at the State University of New York at Binghamton, addresses cultural biases in alcoholism counseling. Specifically, the paper addresses the likely results of counselor cultural bias and lack of sensitivity to the cultural issues for culturally different clients such as incomplete treatment, a poor prognosis for recovery, and the frequency of relapse.

In the final paper, Professor Margery A. Neely of Kansas State University, addresses the dyadic interaction between White counselors in predominantly White colleges and Black students using intergroup contact theory. Methods of reducing the mutual stereotyping in such relationships are discussed.

When Being Different Isn't Funny

Larry C. Loesch

Internationally famous comedians have entertained millions of people throughout the world by focusing on the differences in attitudes, cognitions, and behaviors of the peoples of the world. These comedians have been particularly successful in portrayals of individuals who find themselves in situations that are significantly different from their accustomed cultures. The subtlety of the acclaimed comedians' art form is such that they are able to accentuate cultural differences in a manner not generally perceived as offensive. Thus these entertainers do much to facilitate intercultural understandings, and perhaps acceptance.

Most people who are members of cultural minority groups enmeshed in intercultural conflict do not have the ability to use humor as a primary method of reconciliation of difficult situations. When cultural minority persons find themselves, at best, the objects of wonder and curiosity, and, at worst, derision and ridicule, they struggle to find ways to alleviate the stresses of the situation. As facilitators of human understanding and relationships, counselors can help to alleviate the stresses associated with cultural adaptation (Ponterotto & Benesch, 1988). In order to facilitate effective intercultural interpersonal relationships, however, counselors must implement common roles in uncommon ways. Therefore, in order for counselors to be effective in helping cultural minorities to achieve ecological adaptation, they need to realign the focal points of their efforts and to develop new ways of using established skills (Ponterotto & Casas, 1987).

Traditionally, counselors have focused their efforts on emotional, attitudinal, and cognitive processing in clients, based on the assumption that changes in those dynamics will lead to behavioral changes for effective ecological adaptations. Although such approaches are generally effective, they require relatively long periods of time for implementation. Unfortunately cultural minorities typically do not have that much time; they experience substantial stress and distress before effective behavior change results from "traditional" counseling interventions. Indeed, behavioral differences are often a crucial component of cultural minorities' adjustment difficulties (Furst, 1988). Moreover, attempts to change cultural minority persons' emotional, attitudinal, and cognitive processing may *add* to the psychological stresses they experience. Therefore, counselors can best facilitate ecological adaptation more efficiently by focusing on behavior changes and assuming that attitudinal and cognitive changes will follow. It follows that a primary role of counselors is to help cultural minority persons identify and establish those behaviors likely to lead to ecological adaptation as rapidly as possible.

The intercultural adaptation difficulties with which counselors may be confronted are myriad, and accordingly so are the roles which they may assume to attempt to alleviate those difficulties. Clearly, complete discussion of possible roles is beyond the scope of this presentation. Therefore, only four "broad" roles are addressed herein. These include counselors' roles as (a) promoters of intercultural understanding, (b) counselors, (c) resource consultants, and (d) "reality markers."

The Counselor as Promoter of Intercultural Understanding

A distinguishing feature of the counseling profession is its developmental (preventative) emphasis. Far more than other helping professionals, counselors are involved in activities intended to help persons alleviate problems before they occur.

Persons newly ensconced in an intercultural situation differ from the "majority culture" in many ways. Among the more obvious differences are speech and language behaviors. However, equally important are differences in kinesic (body movement), proxemic (physical space), artifactual (dress), haptic (touch), and paralanguage (accent) behaviors. Collectively, these are the behaviors that make the cultural minority person "different," and therefore they should be the focus of counselors' developmental activity efforts designed to promote intercultural acceptance.

Traditionally, counselors' developmental activities have been primarily in educational systems. For the most part these activities have been successful (Myrick, 1988). Unfortunately, however, they have not been focused often enough on ecological adaptation issues and concerns. Given the increasing frequency with which ecological adaptation situations are occurring in an increasingly mobile world community, such emphasis is certainly warranted. Although school counselors should conduct activities intended to help children to understand their feelings and attitudes about cultural differences in both verbal and noverbal behaviors, they should also help children develop behaviors that enable them to interact positively and effectively with cultural minority children.

Unfortunately, counselors in other than educational settings have done far too little developmental work in general, and in regard to facilitation of intercultural interpersonal relationships in particular. Developmental activities similar to those needed in schools also should be conducted for adults across the life span.

The Counselor as Counselor

Many cultural minority persons are reluctant to seek counseling even in the face of significant adjustment difficulties (Vacc, Wittmer, & DeVaney, 1988). Therefore, counselors often cannot be counselors to cultural minority persons unless they are proactive in the provision of counseling services. Certainly counselors should not be uninvited "intruders" in the lives of cultural minority persons, but, just as certainly, their services often will not be sought unless they make them easily available, both psychologically and physically, to cultural minority persons. Thus, developing ways that are psychologically comfortable to cultural minority persons to receive counseling services is an important role for counselors.

Before counselors can become effective multicultural counseling service providers, they must first adapt a role as "intercultural learner" (Ponterotto & Casas, 1987). Ill-informed counselors actually have a strong potential for making matters worse for their cultural minority clients (Parker, 1988).

The nature of the services provided to cultural minority persons are contingent upon several factors. Of primary concern are the nature of the client's problem(s) and the associated factor of whether the counselor is competent to provide counseling services to help with the particular problem(s). Another related factor is the type(s) of counseling service(s) the client is willing to accept or participate in for help with the problem(s). Again, evaluation of these factors and their influences on counseling processes is to a large extent contingent upon the counselor's knowledge and intercultural awareness.

In the provision of counseling services, counselors will most likely be effective if they concentrate on the identification and evaluation of *behaviors* likely to be effective for their cultural minority clients in efficiently achieving ecological adaptation. The most efficient way for cultural minority persons to achieve comfortable adaptation is for them to *act* in adaptive ways. However, not all ways of behaving identified will be acceptable to clients. Therefore, another significant role for counselors is to help cultural minority persons to develop skills to evaluate the appropriateness of their behaviors.

The Counselor as Resource Consultant

One of the most difficult tasks cultural minority persons confront when attempting to integrate effectively into a majority culture is the identification of effective resources, including those encompassed in a range from daily living needs to psychological adjustment needs. By virtue of training, counselors should be effective "resource persons" for cultural minorities (Ibrahim & Arrendondo, 1986).

In the resource utilization context, counselors' intercultural knowledge must extend beyond characteristics, traits, and behavior patterns of cultural minority clients to include skills as potential resource providers. Because counselors can and should act as liaisons between clients and resource providers, they must know how resource providers generally react to solicitations for resources. It does no good for a counselor to put a cultural minority client in contact with a resource provider if the resource provider is unwilling or unable to provide the resources.

The counselor's role as a resource consultant involves two major components. The first and most important, and also the most frequently minimized, is determining whether the cultural minority client actually wants resource consultation assistance. The second component is determining the most appropriate way(s) for a cultural minority client to seek resource assistance. Counselors can and should help clients to set priorities. They should then assist cultural minority clients with determining the nature and sequence of behaviors that are most likely to result in achieving the desired resources.

The Counselor as Reality Marker

Perhaps the most unique role of counselors in their efforts to assist cultural minority persons to achieve effective ecological adaptation is to act as "reality markers." The term "reality markers" is used here to mean persons to whom cultural minority persons can turn for open, honest, and objective feedback on their current or intended behaviors. In effect, counselors in this role serve as caring members of the cultural majority who aspire to assist cultural minority persons to adjust within the majority culture with a minimum of stress and distress.

Counselors can engage in a wide variety of activities to fulfill this role, but two are most common. The first is simply engaging in nonthreatening or nondisparaging conversation with cultural minority persons. Persons in situations where they are a cultural minority will have many questions about what behavior is appropriate. Counselors, because of their interpersonal skills and caring attitudes, are excellent resources to provide answers to those questions.

The second common activity in which counselors can engage to help cultural minority persons adjust is behavior rehearsal. That is, counselors can allow cultural minority persons to "try out" new behaviors in a "psychologically safe" environment, one free from derision, before they exhibit those behaviors in the majority culture. For example, counselors can provide feedback on different modes of dress, new ways of greeting other people, meanings of gestures, or varieties of "socially acceptable" behaviors. In effect, counselors become the "reality" standard against which cultural minority persons can judge their real or intended behaviors. A note of caution must be interjected at his point. Although counselors can serve in an extremely valuable and helpful capacity as "reality markers," they should assume such roles only if requested to do so.

Conclusion

Most of the time, being a cultural minority person is "no laughing matter." Although it would be nice if people could "laugh their troubles away," most people cannot, and cultural minority persons are no exceptions to that general rule. Thus, most cultural minority persons are in need of assistance from others in order to achieve effective ecological adaptation. Counselors typically have characteristics, skills, and abilities that make them uniquely suited to provide such assistance effectively. To do so they must use their common, established skills and knowledge in uncommon ways. If they are effective in their efforts, both cultural minority and majority persons will benefit. Perhaps then instead of laughing at one another because of our differences, we can all laugh together.

References

Furst, J.M. (1988). Immigrant children in U.S. public schools: Challenges with solutions. *Phi Delta Kappan, 70*(3), 205–210.

Ibrahim, F.A., & Arrendondo, P.A. (1986). Ethical standards for cross-cultural counseling: Counselor preparation, practice, assessment, and research. *Journal or Counseling and Development, 64*(5), 349–352.

Myrick, R.D. (1988). *Developmental guidance and counseling: A practical approach.* Minneapolis, MN: Educational Media Corporation.

Parker, W.M. (1988). *Consciousness raising: A primer for multicultural counseling.* Springfield, IL: Charles C Thomas.

Ponterotto, J.G., & Benesch, K.F. (1988). An organizational framework for understanding the role of culture in counseling. *Journal of Counseling and Development, 66*(5), 237–241.

Ponterotto, J.G., & Casas, J.M. (1987). In search of multicultural competence within counselor education programs. *Journal of Counseling and Development, 65*(8), 430–434.

Vacc, N.A., Wittmer, J., & DeVaney, S. (1988). *Experiencing and counseling multicultural and diverse populations.* Muncie, IN: Accelerated Development.

The Role of Counselors in Combating the "New Racism" at Predominantly White Universities

Donelda A. Cook and Janet E. Helms

A resurgence of overt racist acts committed toward Black students at predominantly White institutions (PWIs) in the United States has gained attention in the national media during the past 2 years. *The Chronicle of Higher Education*, national newspapers, popular (e.g., *Ebony, Essence*) and news magazines (e.g., *Newsweek*), as well as national television programs (e.g., *Frontline*) have reported on the prevalence of racial harassment and violence occurring on major university campuses. Elite Ivy League institutions of the Northeast, "Big 10" universities of the Midwest, state colleges of the South, and universities embedded in the liberal tradition of the West all share headlines of "racism on the university campus."

Concerned educators are addressing the issue of the "new" racism on college campuses (Farrell, 1988). It is new in the Black Americans are no longer fighting for the right to attend White universities, but Black students are finding that often White campuses are hostile environments that harbor sentiments of "old" racism. Black college students are stunned by overt acts of racism such as cross-burnings, mob attacks, and racial slurs aired publicly via university radio stations and other communications systems.

Institutional Interventions

The public notoriety of overt racist activities has prompted some universities to begin addressing the issue of racial harassment. University-centered efforts have ranged from "studies" of the problem of racism on the campus to recruitment strategies for attracting Black faculty and students.

Counselors can become involved at the institutional level by assuming the role of an "environmental consultant." Counselors who have been trained to examine the person-environment interaction are in a position to educate the university community about the sociocultural implications of racism on campus. Counselors have been called upon to provide racism-sensitivity workshops for faculty, staff, and students. In addition, counselors can assist university administrators in understanding the psychological manifestations of racism from the perspectives of the oppressor and the oppressed. In this way, administrators can learn to recognize their own fears of being called "racist" and feelings of guilt in acknowledging their own racist attitudes. Once university officials are able to understand the socialization process of institutional racism in the United States and to move beyond the affective responses to racism, they can begin to develop a plan to include effective problem-solving strategies.

The university-centered solutions to the problem, however, take time to develop and implement. In reality they may have minimal impact on the psychological functioning of Black students at PWIs. Educators must consider what Black students have endured prior to the problem of racism that has resulted in media coverage. Black students at PWIs have historically been oppressed by covert racial cues within the university environment such as (a) "institutional constraints" of limited funding for African-American studies and academic retention programs; (b) scarcity of Black faculty to serve as role models; and (c) high attrition rates due to financial pressures. Socially, Black students have experienced racist themes at White fraternity parties, differential treatment by White professors, and racial incidents in campus housing (Farrell, 1988). The overall neglect of racial diversity exhibited on White campuses relays a message that "Black presence" at PWIs is not valued nor encouraged.

Outreach to Black Students

Displays of cultural and racial insensitivity within the university serve to undermine the self-esteem and confidence of Black students and ultimately influence their successful matriculation. Comparison studies of Black and White students at predominantly

White universities have found that "social estrangement" is a contributing factor to the attrition of Black students (Suen, 1983) and to their progress (e.g., earned fewer credits, stayed fewer quarters), whereas this was not found to be an issue for White students (Lunnenborg & Lunnenborg, 1985).

Other studies have revealed more specific evidence of the psychological impact of racism on Black students. For instance, Black students perceived that they faced more academic difficulties than their White counterparts, in part because of the energy required to adapt to a different class and cultural situation, which takes time and mental concentration from academic pursuits (Loo & Rolison, 1986). Some Black students reported responding to racist attitudes or actions by isolating themselves socially and feeling discouraged from seeking academic help from faculty and teaching assistants or working cooperatively with White students (Lewis, 1987).

Counselors can intervene in support of Black students through outreach activities, particularly utilizing group interventions. Open-ended support groups can help to facilitate a sense of unity among Black students and provide a cathartic experience for them, thus combating their feelings of social isolation. Theme-oriented groups that focus on aspects of African-American culture can help students develop positive racial identity. Skills-oriented groups can be conducted to teach Black students how to recognize, confront, and cope with racist attitudes and behaviors in their environment. Such groups can be effective in helping Black students to distinguish between isolated acts of racism and viewing the entire campus as racist, thus enabling Black students to utilize the campus resources that are available to them.

Individual Counseling to Black Students

Other studies have provided information that can be helpful to counselors working individually with students. In a comparison study (Fleming, 1985) of Blacks attending PWIs and those attending historically Black colleges, it was found that Black students attending PWIs experienced obstacles in their adjustment, including feelings of alienation, disengagement from academic involvement, and futile attempts at finding ways of asserting themselves. Some students responded to the inhospitable climate by becoming rebellious, whereas others acquiesced. The psychological impact of racism seems further confounded when Black students are blind to the external circumstances of racism and consequently internalize the oppression. That is, those students who do not recognize that they are being treated unjustly due to their race often blame themselves for the circumstances. This results in depression, withdrawal, avoidance, self-defeating behaviors, misdirected anger, and generally maladaptive problem-solving behaviors for surviving in a hostile environment. These students are likely to seek counseling with presenting problems of lack of motivation, test anxiety, stress, physical symptoms, or other academic problems emanating from maladaptive coping strategies.

The counselor's role in individual counseling with Black students can be one of providing systemic support, reality testing, education, and advocacy. Counselors need to support the students in their "right" to be at the university and communicate faith in their ability to succeed. Often students need to be confronted with the consequences of their self-defeating behaviors, whether it is isolating themselves socially, poor study habits, or cutting classes. For a student who does not recognize that he or she is a victim of racism, it is necessary to explore the circumstances of the presenting problem in specific detail to determine whether he or she has encountered a racial incident. If so, the counselor may have to help the student understand the problem from a sociocultural perspective rather than one of self-blame. The counselor can then work through the emotional response with the student and teach the student more adaptive coping strategies for surviving in a racist environment.

Counselors can also be helpful in serving as advocates for their counselees. In instances where a student has encountered a traumatic racial incident, it may be effective for the counselor to intervene with faculty or academic advisors on behalf of the student. Many students respond to harassment or discrimination through the use of denial. Consequently, by the time the students seek counseling, their maladaptive coping behaviors may have affected their academic performance. Counselors should view the psychological stress of coping with racism as they would any other forms of victimization. That is, if a counselor would intervene in helping a student to withdraw from a class, take an "incomplete" in a class, or make up an exam due to the psychological trauma of being a victim of other societal ills (e.g., sexual harassment, psychological abuse), so should be the case with victims of traumatic incidents of racism. Even though racial harassment is a difficult issue to confirm legally, counselors must not let that interfere with their responsiveness to its psychological impact on their clients, and they should use their power within the university to support Black students in their efforts to cope with institutional racism.

In conclusion, racism is a societal problem and it does exist in our institutions of higher education. University counselors can assume various roles in combating the "new racism" at predominantly White universities. This paper has outlined three such roles: (1) serving as environmental consultants in educating the perpetrators of the problem, (2) implementing outreach programs to empower Black students through group cohesiveness and positive racial identity development, and (3) supporting and educating Black students through individual counseling and serving as their advocates so that they might become survivors of the problem of institutional racism.

References

Farrell, C.S. (1988). Black students seen facing "new racism" on many campuses. *The Chronicle of Higher Education, 37*(20), Al.

Fleming, J. (1985). *Blacks in college.* San Francisco: Jossey-Bass.

Lewis, S. (1987). Race relations on campus: The problem, some solutions. *Technology Review, 90,* 4–9.

Loo, C.M., & Rolison, G. (1986). Alienation of ethnic minority students at a predominantly White university. *Journal of Higher Education, 57,* 58–77.

Lunnenborg, P.W., & Lunnenborg, C.E. (1985). Student centered versus university-centered solutions to problems of minority students. *Journal of College Student Personnel, 26,* 224–228.

Suen, H.K. (1983). Alienation and attrition of Black college students on a predominantly White campus. *Journal of College Student Personnel, 24,* 117–121.

Cultural Bias in Alcoholism Counseling

Robert Jacque Chapman

Alcoholism counseling literature has been dominated by articles concerning theory and the application of technique in the intervention with and treatment of the alcoholic patient. Such have been primarily postulated by a White middle class counseling establishment, as is the case with most literature on psychotherapy (Pedersen, 1981, 1987). To this end, culturally different clients have not fared well with such approaches to counseling in general (Sue, 1981) and alcoholism counseling specifically. From the early 1960s come the beginning reports of the counseling profession's failure to adequately serve the culturally different.

This lack of cultural sensitivity in counseling has included the mistaken belief that counseling is the preferred mode of intervention to assist individuals in all cases of maladaptive behavior. Recently the Western counselor has begun to realize that counseling and psychotherapy are merely representative of the many approaches to providing mental health services worldwide (Das, 1987; Pedersen, 1981, 1987).

In light of these facts, counselor perceptions of patient progress in treatment are often influenced by that counselor's personal cultural perspective or bias. When addressing the problems of alcoholism, with its high incidence of denial and low levels of commitment to abstinence, the issue of cultural bias becomes significant when evaluating the treatment needs and progress of the culturally different client.

When the counselor encounters the distinct values and beliefs of the culturally different client with alcoholism, cultural bias may well result in the counselor's perception of denial. Unfortunately, such bias invites misperception and a resulting misdiagnosis that contribute to an ineffective approach to treatment.

An example can be illustrated by considering a frequently used therapeutic response to denial: the counselor directed model of intervention (Johnson, 1980). The Johnson model is a typical technique employed by alcoholism counselors in order to affect perceived denial. This approach has the counselor coordinate a specific and intentional intervention with an alcoholic family. The expressed purpose is to guide the family in its caring but firm confrontation of the person with alcoholism. The resulting effect is to offer the family an appropriate way to respond to the illness and its impact on them specifically and the family in general (Johnson, 1980).

When used to confront a culturally biased perception of denial, such an approach leads to frustrated clinical relationships as exemplified by failed appointments and prematurely terminated treatment and to disappointing therapeutic results as well. This clinical problem is further exacerbated by the counselor's attempt to direct the culturally different family to intervene in the disease process. A counselor-initiated attempt to orchestrate a family intervention (Johnson, 1980) may only serve to suggest that the family abandon its traditional values regarding familial roles. An example is seen in the Latino family with an alcoholic father. In an intervention, the family is placed in a position of choosing between the traditional cultural value of "respecto" or familial respect shown toward elders and the counselor-directed intervention. The following specific examples illustrate the existence of cultural bias in alcoholism counseling.

1. *The alcoholism counselor holds monocultural assumptions with resulting stereotypical views.* The counselors' dogmatic acceptance of the stereotypical beliefs of the dominant culture promotes a view that the resolution of problems in treatment for the culturally different is the responsibility of the client. Such an approach increases the likelihood of problems in such a clinical relationship with a culturally different client.

An example is when the culturally different counselor expects the alcoholic client to be prompt for each session. Because of a culturally based difference in the value placed upon promptness, a client with alcoholism may be consistently late for scheduled appointments. Such behavior may be interpreted by the culturally different counselor as disinterest in counseling and contribute to the counselor's perception of patient denial and affect the evaluation of the client's progress in therapy. In actuality, such tardiness results from the client's interest in other events in the present that are perceived as more important than the scheduled appointment. This is frequently experienced when treating Native Americans who hold strong beliefs regarding the importance of the temporal present and a commitment to such values (Richardson, 1981). Consistent tardiness is often misinterpreted by the counselor unfamiliar with culturally different perceptions of time. This tardiness is then seen as indicative of the patient's limited commitment to therapy or characteristic of active denial and indicative of the need for direct and specific confrontation.

2. *Insensitivity to the cultural variations among individuals and the assumption that the counselor's perception of life corresponds to reality.* This bias not only adds to the counselor's difficulty in establishing a relationship with a culturally different alcoholic client, but significantly increases the likelihood that a misperception of denial or a lack of commitment to treatment will result in an ineffective or unnecessary intervention. To expand upon the example cited in number 1, being consistently late or missing scheduled appointments may not only influence the counselor's evaluation of the client's progress in therapy, but influence the counselor's diagnostic impressions of that client. Such an evaluation of client tardiness finds the clinician weighing the benefits of intervention against termination of the client for lack of commitment ot therapy.

3. *Counselor-perceived resistance to treatment.* The acceptance of stereotypical assumptions about counseling, its outcome, and appropriate client responses increases the likelihood that the counselor will perceive a resistance to treatment when the client resists therapeutic suggestions.

This is illustrated when the counselor believes that passive verbal acceptance of treatment goals and objectives without active follow-through is indicative of denial and must be confronted promptly. When such a belief is accepted without confirmation, the counselor may implement a traditional therapeutic response of intervention (Johnson, 1980), before exploring the possible cultural bases for the perceived client behavior.

A classic example can be seen when the culturally insensitive counselor encounters the Native American client. Being unfamiliar with the traditional Native American value of maintaining a posture of noninvolvement and avoiding behavior that could be construed as attention seeking, the counselor perceives resistance to treatment in the behavior of the client who refrains from active participation in group or individual counseling (Richardson, 1981; Trimble, 1981).

4. *Cultural bias and a counselor's dogmatic adherence to a specific treatment modality.* Cultural bias in this example reduces counselor sensitivity to specific client issues and

increases the likelihood of treatment being dictated by a diagnosis based upon the misperception of cultural difference as pathology.

As noted frequently in this article, the counselor will perceive denial and a low commitment to treatment when encountering the personal values of the culturally different client. This perception invites a standard response to such patient behavior through confrontation; however, the clinical focus is then placed on treating the alcoholism rather than the client who happens to have alcoholism.

A case in point; a 45-year-old male Native American who, on being questioned in group therapy about the consequences of his drinking, assumes a nonassertive posture of no eye contact, silence, and apparent emotional withdrawal. Such is perceived by the counselor unfamiliar with traditional Native American values as denial and fatalism and therefore in need of direct confrontation by the group. The confrontation results in no measurable change in the client's disclosures. As a result, the counselor recommends to staff that the client in question be discharged from treatment for reasons of noncompliance with treatment.

A discharge does not take place. The counselor is presented with the salient cultural issues in effect in this case with the recommendation that issues of individual concern for the counselor in this client's treatment be addressed in individual counseling. When the recommended changes in treatment strategy are implemented, the client is able to successfully complete treatment. These four examples give rise to a fifth, which is the most pervasive of all examples of cultural bias in alcoholism counseling.

5. *Clinical arrogance.* This bias is exemplified by a tendency to attribute the difficulties in counseling the culturally different client with alcoholism to the client. The problems encountered in counseling the culturally different alcoholic client are exacerbated by the counselor's cultural bias and apparent unwillingness to address salient cultural issues. The client often ends treatment prematurely, frequently after the first interview. Such behavior serves to confirm a perception of denial and resistance to treatment. Clinical arrogance attributes all problems in therapy to the client. As a result, recommendations are made for direct and confrontive measures to impact the perceived denial. Examples of such measures may include the termination of social service benefits, incarceration, termination of employment, or the placement of children in foster care. Confrontation is effective in addressing genuine resistance to treatment; if a client's behavior, however, is culturally motivated rather than denial, confrontation only serves to reinforce the client's perception of institutional racism.

Practical alcoholism treatment experience with culturally different clients, together with a review of the cross-cultural counseling literature, leads to eight suggestions for the culturally different alcoholism counselor in order to avoid what Wrenn (1962) referred to as cultural encapsulation.

1. *To note that the client with alcoholism may hold stereotypical views that are applied to the counselor from the dominant culture.* Such a realization will enable the alcoholism counselor to prepare for the issue of distrust held by many patients for their culturally different counselor (Deloria, 1983; Dinges, Trimble, Manson, & Pasquale, 1983; Lockart, 1981). The counselor can avoid the hasty perception that client hesitation, steeped in distrust, is indicative of denial and/or resistance to treatment.

2. *To acknowledge one's lack of familiarity with the cultural values of the alcoholic patient.* The client probably assumes that the culturally different counselor is unfamiliar with the client's culture (Deloria, 1983). Many professionals fail to learn about the various

cultural values of their patients, not to mention the importance of counselor sensitivity to the issues of counseling across cultures. This results in one or more of the following:

a. A general lack of understanding of the client's native culture;
b. Counselor retention of stereotypical cultural views of the client; and
c. The use of standardized techniques and approaches to treatment with all clients, regardless of their cultural background.

On those occasions where a clinician works or lives close to the environment from which the culturally different client comes, it can be both helpful and enlightening to familiarize him- or herself with the culture of the client. The author, when working on a Native American reservation, frequently attended the festivals or "doins," as they were referred to locally. These exposures to the values and customs of the reservation result in a better appreciation for and sensitivity to the issues affecting the lives of clients being treated.

3. *To recognize that all barriers to treatment are not indicative of client resistance or denial of alcoholism.* Although direct and confrontive intervention is an effective method of addressing genuine denial (Johnson, 1980), the counselor is well advised to confirm the denial, in part by ruling out cultural bias, before proceeding with plans to confront.

4. *To become aware of the need to determine treatment based upon client issues.* It is inappropriate to hastily assign treatment strategy to observed client behaviors and the culturally biased clinical evaluation of such (Pedersen, 1987). To treat the alcoholism rather than to treat the person who has the alcoholism renders the clinician prone to a display of cultural insensitivity and bias. Consequently, this focus on the illness results in a clinician's greater interest in technique than the real issues and needs of the client. The provision of treatment in such a way will only serve to confirm a suspicious client's expectation of institutional racism.

5. *To speak and share openly with the culturally different patient displaying an attitude of respect* (Youngman & Sodongei, 1983). Lewis and Ho (1983), in referring to Native Americans, stated that a worker who shows respect for the system, values, and norms of the client eventually places him- or herself in a position of trust and credibility.

6. *To avoid giving advice.* Most alcoholic patients tend to see their culturally different counselor as interested in quick answers and easy solutions. To pursue such answers and solutions serves to confirm the client's cultural biases around the counselor's tendency to dominate, with little respect for the cultural values of the client (Lewis & Ho, 1983; Lockart, 1981).

7. *To avoid the hasty expectation of results in therapy.* Counseling that has as its primary intent to quickly assess the client, formulate a diagnostic impression, articulate a treatment strategy, and proceed according to that strategy, often serves to confirm if not exacerbate the culturally biased opinions many clients hold for their culturally different counselor (Lockart, 1981).

8. *To recognize that an alcoholism counselor should not be preoccupied with seeing through a client's denial, but rather seeing the client through treatment.* The anticipation of being taken advantage of by one's client may lead the counselor to see the culturally different values, beliefs, and behaviors of the client as denial. A defensive posture by a counselor plus a lack of sensitivity to the important cultural issues of the client certainly results in difficulty in counseling the culturally different client with alcoholism.

Concluding Remarks

An initial review of these suggestions may seem to support the belief that a culturally different client may best be served by arranging for the client to work with a culturally similar counselor. This is not this author's recommendation. Rather, the interests of therapy with culturally different alcoholic patients are best served when counselor sensitivity to the relevant cultural issues concerning the client is coupled with professional skill, proficiency, technique (Acosta & Sheehan, 1976; Atkinson, Marayama, & Matsui, 1978), and a thorough understanding of alcoholism as an illness.

As issues of cultural bias are addressed and the alcoholism counselor is successful in preventing cultural encapsulation (Wrenn, 1962), the results of therapy with culturally different clients with alcoholism are significantly improved.

An awareness of the importance of cultural sensitivity in the counseling relationship will enhance the outcome of therapy. Approaching treatment in such a way may well work better than to attempt to match a client with a culturally similar counselor who has been trained in techniques of the White middle class counseling establishment (Pedersen, 1981) and assimilated into the dominant culture.

References

Acosta, F., & Sheehan, J. (1976). Preferences toward Mexican American and Anglo American psychotherapists. *Journal of Consulting and Clinical Psychology, 44,* 272–279.

Atkinson, D.R., Marayama, M., & Matsui, S. (1978). Effects of counselor race and counseling approach on Asian Americans' perception of counselor credibility and utility. *Journal of Counseling Psychology, 25,* 76–83.

Das, A.K. (1987). Indigenous models of therapy in traditional Asian societies. *Journal of Multicultural Counseling and Development, 15,* 25–37.

Deloria, V. (1983). Indians today, the real and unreal. In D.R. Atkinson, G. Morten, & D.W. Sue (Eds.), *Counseling American minorities: A cross cultural perspective* (2nd ed.) (pp. 47–64). Dubuque, IA: W.C. Brown.

Dinges, N.G., Trimble, J.E., Manson, S.M., & Pasquale, F.L. (1983). Counseling and psychotherapy with American Indians and Alaskan Natives. In A.J. Marsella, & P.B. Pedersen (Eds.), *Cross cultural counseling and psychotherapy* (2nd ed.). University of Hawaii: Pergamon Press.

Johnson, V. (1980). *I'll quit tomorrow* (rev. ed.). New York: Harper & Row.

Lewis, R.G., & Ho, M.K. (1983). Social work with Native Americans. In D.R. Atkinson, G. Morten, & D.W. Sue (Eds.), *Counseling American minorities: A cross cultural perspective* (2nd ed.) (pp. 65–72) Dubuque, IA: W.C. Brown.

Lockart, B. (1981). Historic distrust and the counseling of American Indians and Alaskan Natives. *White Cloud Journal,* 2(3).

Pedersen, P.B. (1981). The cultural inclusiveness of counseling. In P.B. Pedersen, J.G. Dragons, W.J. Lonner, & J.G. Dragons (Eds.), *Counseling across cultures* (2nd ed.). Honolulu: The University of Hawaii Press.

Pedersen, P.B. (1987). Ten frequent assumptions of cultural bias in counseling. *Journal of Multicultural Counseling and Development, 15,* 16–24.

Richardson, E.H. (1981). Cultural and historic perspectives in counseling American Indians. In D.W. Sue, *Counseling the culturally different.* New York: Wiley.

Sue, D.W. (1981). *Counseling the culturally different,* New York: Wiley.

Trimble, J.E. (1981). Value differentials and their importance in counseling American Indians. In P.B. Pedersen, J.G. Dragons, W.J. Lonner, & J.E. Trimble (Eds.), *Counseling across cultures* (2nd ed.). Honolulu: The University of Hawaii Press.

Wrenn, G.C. (1962). The culturally encapsulated counselor. *Harvard Educational Review, 32*(4), 444–449.

Youngman, G., & Sodongei, M. (1983). Counseling the American Indian child. In D.R. Atkinson, G. Morten, & D.W. Sue (Eds.), *Counseling American minorities: A cross cultural perspective* (2nd ed.). Dubuque, IA: W. C. Brown.

Intergroup Contact Theory: White Counselors and Black Students

Margery A. Neely

Intergroup Contact Theory

Intergroup contact theory and research grew out of early work on prejudice by focusing on social attitudes of one group toward another in the military, housing projects, and industry, and later extended to school desegregation issues, (Stephan & Brigham, 1985). Findings indicated that certain core conditions, when present, fostered enhanced intergroup contact: (1) support by authority figures for egalitarianism; (2) equal status in the contact setting; (3) cooperative interdependence; (4) setting that enhances perception of outgroup members as individuals; and (5) personal attributes that disconfirm categorical stereotypes (Rothbart & John, 1985; Stephan & Brigham, 1985).

The initial research on changing attitudes emphasized the nature of the contact situation between ingroups and outgroups but paid little attention to factors within individuals or the goal of the contact that affects outcomes. Both situational and individual factors are important (Brewer & Kramer, 1985) in settings such as university campuses where minority students must seek help of White professionals in counseling/ teaching/advising. Most situations violate the conditions needed to improve intergroup relations (Brewer & Kramer, 1985; Rothbart & John, 1985).

Of interest in intergroup contact theory is that stereotyping—categorization—is not seen as an emotionally negative value or myth, but as a typical variable of cognitive/ affective connotations of intergroup contact. The contact hypothesis literature, as well as findings representative of the White counselor-Black client research from the past 20 years, is relevant to issues of intergroup contact.

Support by Authority Figures

Counselors, and other advisors, are agents of the institution, *supported by the authority of the system,* to deliver specific, expert personal aid to all students. Three of the five factors are present for favorable contact outcomes in support given by authority figures—but predominantly White campuses in predominantly White states do not provide many opportunities for homegrown counselors to interact with Black students as *individuals* or colleagues. Thus, *personal attributes that could disconfirm categorical stereotypes* are likely to be little observed.

On the part of the Black student, preference for a Black counselor/advisor over a White counselor/advisor may or may not exist (Atkinson, 1987), may or may not be related to the type of problem (Thompson & Cimbolic, 1978), and may or may not be related to the stage of racial identity of either party (Helms, 1986). These inconsistencies in research on cross-cultural dyads may in part be explained by intergroup contact theory.

Equal Status

Brewer and Kramer (1985) pointed out that equal status in the contact setting has to take into account both historical status differences and immediate status differences as determinants of intergroup acceptance. Yet, because the powerless outgroup (student) tends to know more about the ingroup (counselor) than vice versa (Rothbart & John, 1985), the client acts upon more information in suspending judgment.

In a helping session between a White professional and a Black client, the values upheld as being right are usually those of the powerful White majority (Boyer, 1988; Butler, 1987; Carter, 1988). Among other conditions of contact leading to anxiety, the White professionals have higher status and may regard the minority student as inferior, fear resentment, feel guilty about their own advantaged position, or justify the advantaged status by disdaining the lower-status member (Stephan & Stephan, 1985). High anxiety levels of White professionals who have little prior contact with members of another race are likely to amplify usual behavioral responses, biases, public or private self-awareness, emotional reactions, and evaluations of the other group's members (Stephan & Stephan).

The lower status minority students bring their educational and historical experiences with them and may anticipate inferior treatment or exploitation (Sedlacek, 1987), resent high-status group members, worry about showing that resentment, or fear interaction because they regard themselves as inferior.

Yet Black students also bring strengths from their experiences (Atkinson, 1987; Butler, 1987; Helms, 1984; Sedlacek, 1987; Sue, 1988). Moreover, they can anticipate that agents of the institution are not going to use their positions for overt exploitation (Simons, Berkowitz, & Moyer, 1970): a "benign" circle is established because institutions desperate for Black student enrollment numbers provide students with power (Weigel & Howes, 1985).

Cooperative Interdependence

The goals within the interaction could be similar for both parties once rapport is established (Atkinson, 1987; Stephan & Stephan, 1985). However, the noncognitive variables that Sedlacek (1987) reviewed as important to Black students' success in higher education reveal differences in process and goals that might contribute to difficulties in establishing movement toward goals. The White counselor may not choose the same steps that the Black client would as being feasible ways to reach a goal (Sedlacek, 1987).

A working alliance, *a cooperative effort,* ensues during which the goals are to solve or resolve the student's problem. One problem arises from the definitions of mental health and mental illness as taught in training programs based upon White, male, middle-class norms. Not only are the Black/White worldviews different, but also the perception of what constitutes a "problem" and how that perception is derived.

In contrast, when cultural similarity is perceived, it tends to override a racial label in terms of attraction and social distance in situations with low social pressure and no intergroup competition (Brewer & Kramer, 1985). Heppner and Heesacker (1982) found that counselors rated as attractive indicated they had more therapeutic power over clients over time (race of client not indicated).

When middle-class values are held or where many interactions with the outgroup have been the norm, the Black/White dyad does not pose so much of a threat. This conclusion is supported by findings that no association with race in found, but similarity of attitude is, in successful outcomes of counseling (Atkinson, 1987), although some relationship to socioeconomic status differences is linked to degree of similarity of attitudes. Black students, moreover, value help from an understanding professional.

Individuation

To effect positive change, the counselor in the ideal counseling relationship must develop initial rapport through warmth, focus on the here and now, display respect, genuineness, and unconditional positive regard, and employ active listening skills. These techniques are thought to reduce feelings of anxiety in the client and help the client feel at ease with the counselor and disclose problems because the professional is an expert as well as a gatekeeper of information (Ewing, 1974). In anxiety-producing situations, however, expected behaviors will be noticed whereas small deviations are unnoticed, and, if noticed, will be attributed to some subordinate category.

The counseling relationship as it develops becomes informal, intimate, and unpleasant: Behaviors are associated with such situations that differ from situations described by the opposite adjectives—formal, distant, or pleasant. Both client and counselor may struggle with the intimacy inherent in an involving, as opposed to a noninvolving, interaction; formal situations result in more superficial behavior and produce less anxiety (Stephan & Stephan, 1985).

Although the literature is not clear, Black students have been found to: prefer White counselors on issues involving advocacy for themselves (Gibbs, 1975); drop out more often from sessions with White counselors; show no differences in preference for self-disclosure of problems to Black or White counselors; self-disclose to female counselors more personally relevant materials; self-disclose more to culturally sensitive counselors depending on degree of racial identity (Helms, 1986), with facilitative level co-varied; engage in self-exploration more with White counselors than with Black; but overall deem counseling competence the most important variable (Harrison, 1975).

A Black student's willingness for a White counselor to be privy to a problem that cannot be discussed with the family requires that the contact episode must overcome stereotypes that both hold. For example, gender-role struggles among male and female

Blacks are undergoing changes similar to those in White male and female gender roles and socialization. Thus, talking to an opposite-sex counselor can, in this case, exacerbate the difficulties in talking with an opposite-race counselor.

Disconfirmation of Stereotypes

The Black student is in the counseling/advising session not as a representative of Black students but as someone selected independent of the category "Black"—meaning that the counselor will be more likely to change any unfavorable assumptions more easily (Brewer & Kramer, 1985; Rothbart & John, 1985). This finding of the intergroup contact theory perhaps explains some of the cynicism by Whites toward quotas in admissions and hiring. The lack of selection by category is important because, in general, information being processed is affected by the prevailing category stereotypes—expectations—and the behaviors relevant to those stereotypes are more likely to be remembered. Being unselected allows individuation to occur more quickly so that, for example, professionals do not lower their standards and thereby condescend to minority students.

Summary

In summary, intergroup contact theory suggests that the interaction between White professionals and Black students on predominantly White campuses could be characterized by an initial schema of mutual stereotyping. Fears for proper individual-environment fit can result from strains on the interaction. The contact, to enhance the quality of intergroup interaction and rapport between the minority student and majority professional, should create an intimacy that individuates the participants and disconfirms stereotypic behaviors; is based on equal status; defines cooperation in pursuit of common goals; and provides supportive social norms.

References

Atkinson, D.R. (1987). Counseling black students: A review of the research. *Journal of College Student Personnel, 28,* 562–582.

Boyer, J. (1988). The other side of gender equity: Black males in America. *Educational Considerations, 15,* 15–17.

Brewer, M.B., & Kramer, R.M. (1985). The psychology of intergroup attitudes and behavior. *Annual Review of Psychology, 36,* 219–243.

Butler, A. (1987). *Black girls and schooling.* Manhattan, KS: Kansas State University, Women's Educational Equity Act Program grant, Bluemont Hall, College of Education. (mimeo).

Carter, C. (1988). Black female students: Issues and considerations for teachers of teachers. *Educational Considerations, 15,* 31–36.

Ewing, T. (1974). Racial similarity of client and counselor and client satisfaction with counseling. *Journal of Counseling Psychology, 21,* 446–449.

Gibbs, J.T. (1975). Use of mental health services by black students at a predominantly white university: A three year study. *American Journal of Orthopsychiatry, 45,* 430–445.

Harrison, D.K. (1975). Race as a counselor-client variable in counseling and psychotherapy: A review of the research. *The Counseling Psychologist, 5*(1), 124–133.

Helms, J.E. (1984). Toward a theoretical explanation of the effects of race on counseling: A Black and White model. *Counseling Psychologist, 12*(4), 153–164.

Helms, J.E. (1986). Expanding racial identity theory to cover counseling process. *Journal of Counseling Psychology, 33,* 62–64.

Heppner, P.P., & Heesacker, M. (1982). Interpersonal influence process in real-life counseling: Investigating client perceptions, counselor experience level, and counselor power over time. *Journal of Counseling Psychology, 29,* 215–223.

Rothbart, M., & John, O.P. (1985). Social categorization and behavioral episodes: A cognitive analysis of the effects of intergroup contact. *Journal of Social Issues, 41,* 81–105.

Sedlacek, W.E. (1987). Black students on white campuses: 20 years of research. *Journal of College Student Personnel, 28,* 448–495.

Simons, H.W., Berkowitz, N.N., & Moyer, R.J. (1970). Similarity, credibility, and attitude change: A review and a theory. *Psychological Bulletin, 73,* 1–16.

Stephan, W.G., & Brigham, J.C. (1985). Intergroup contact: Introduction. *Journal of Social Issues, 41,* 1–8.

Stephan, W.G., & Stephan, C.W. (1985). Intergroup anxiety. *Journal of Social Issues, 1,* 157–175.

Sue, D.W. (1978). Eliminating cultural oppression in counseling: Toward a general theory. *Journal of Counseling Psychology, 25,* 419–428.

Sue, S. (1988). Psychotherapeutic services for ethnic minorities: Two decades of research findings. *American Psychologist, 43,* 301–308.

Thompson, R.A., & Cimbolic, P. (1978). Black students' counselor preference and attitudes toward counseling center use. *Journal of Counseling Psychology, 25,* 570–575.

Weigel, R.H., & Howes, P.W. (1985). Conceptions of racial prejudice: Symbolic racism reconsidered. *Journal of Social Issues, 41,* 117–138.

PART IV

POLITICAL ISSUES

Governmental and political institutions create the metaphors as well as the policies and mechanisms by which cultural diversity among citizens is celebrated or seen as troublesome. Dr. Mabel M. Smythe-Haith, former ambassador to the Cameroon and professor emeritus of Northwestern University, speaks from her personal experience in government to the multiple roles counselors can play in dealing with immigrant "newcomers" as well as to culturally different members of society whose ancestry and commitment to the United States or Great Britain spans generations.

Dr. Smythe-Haith speaks to the implications that arise from political diversity and how these are often translated into "local" problems among culturally diverse groups. These issues become the seeds of threat, turfdom, inequality, or a lack of dignity accorded to particular groups of culturally different persons. As such, the "fallout" of these issues becomes the content with which counselors must work in promoting visions of interdependence; helping immigrant groups learn how to negotiate employment, schools, emergencies, and human relations in a new land; facilitating conflict resolution among those who must learn to share power, living space, and opportunities; and providing a map for those who need to negotiate culture shock and acquire alternative cultural competence necessary to compete and progress within American or British society. Dr. Smythe-Haith outlines an agenda for counselors engaged in cross-cultural counseling that needs to be broadly preserved and acted upon in both nations.

The two papers that follow Dr. Smythe-Haith's plenary presentation are examples of how counselors can work with cultural issues that are both political and racial in their contexts. Both papers suggest a cross-cultural counselor role that is productive and flexible in its implementation.

ETHNIC DIVERSITY: THREAT OR OPPORTUNITY?

Mabel M. Smythe-Haith

More than 30 years ago, when I led a group of university students on a study tour of Nigeria, we had a series of adventures in coping with ethnic diversity. We were all very earnest about building bridges to peoples of other cultures, but were not knowledgeable regarding how that might be achieved. Nevertheless, we had great faith in our open-hearted readiness to acknowledge the validity of cultures not our own.

I remember the friendly smiles as our chartered bus drove us carefully through villages unaccustomed to so many unfamiliar visitors and the shouts of what sounded like "Oibo!" from the children lining the road; clearly, we reasoned, that was the local greeting. So we smiled and shouted back, "Oibo!"

We arrived and were greeted by the village chief, who used a local schoolteacher as his interpreter. A few small children edged in and looked shyly at us. So, I thought I would put them at ease. "Oibo!" I said, smiling and stretching out my hand. The chief looked startled and said something to his interpreter who looked at me oddly. "Why are you calling those children White strangers? The chief wants to know," he said. Obviously, understanding something as simple as a greeting has its problems. We make assumptions at our peril; there are always surprises.

Yet, it is our destiny to grow in cultural diversity, to have new languages, new experiences, new groups of people added to those whom we already know or think we do. As the world shrinks and far-away places can be reached in ever fewer travel hours, we find our cities increasingly diverse, rich with the sounds of once-strange languages, with the smells of unfamiliar cuisines, with holiday celebrations and religious observances unknown to us a few years ago. Clothing and hairstyles follow exotic new models; questions are raised about the validity of long-settled customs and practices. Are we changing too fast, without considering all the implications for our values, our future?

Let us pause to reconsider. These is really no question of reversing recent history, taking back London and New York and Hawaiian real estate that was sold thankfully a few years ago to the Arabs or the Japanese or other foreign moguls willing to pay the maximum price at a time when recession or other circumstances had slowed sales to our conventional investors. Getting the genie back into the bottle is not really feasible. For better or worse, we are part of the increasingly international, intercultural, interethnic, interracial world. We cannot proclaim, as did the title of a Broadway musical years ago, "Stop the world! I want to get off!"

Why are we so easily frightened by the prospect of growing diverse in our ethnic origins? Although there is a natural sense of comfort with the familiar and a feeling that homogeneity lacks the rivalries and concern with the zero-sum attitudes that sometimes attend diversity, there are also significant rewards accompanying a polyglot population:

1. Life is clearly more exciting when it offers a smorgasbord of competing philosophies, life-styles, and tastes—all aspects of cultures to examine, experiment with, and enjoy. Our music, our literature, the food we eat, the clothing we wear, the sports we watch (or participate in), our medical and technical achievements—all reflect the richness and diversity of our cultural roots, the genius of the great thinkers of highly varied civilizations. The beauty of the human race benefits from the loveliness of a thousand different features and statures, skin textures and colors, body types, hair arrangements, and styles of clothing and accessories.

2. The genius of the human heart and mind goes beyond its technical brilliance in devising solutions to the problems that plague us; its compassion, its dazzling imagination, its originality, its ability to produce works of genius, insight, and beauty leave us in awe. Yet, we fear the unfamiliar, the strange, the subtle threat inherent in the assumption that the less we know about something, the less we can control it. We fear that our comfortable, accustomed ways will be displaced by unfamiliar ones with people whose ways we do not know and trust and whose appearance, education, and life-style are different from ours—in other words, threatening to our accustomed way of doing things.

We feel threatened by competition in earning a living, in buying housing, in standards of conduct, in school achievement, in standards of beauty or athletic prowess or prosperity in people identified with an unfamiliar ethnic group; at the same time, we are able to accommodate the attribution of limited areas of excellence to a given group we otherwise tend to disparage, as if, for example, we can accept inferior status in assessing female beauty when we can at the same time consider our own group more intelligent, sophisticated, or destined for leadership. A similar trade-off occurs when a mother accepts the superiority of her son's playmate in school achievement if she values sufficiently her perception that her own child is more handsome.

A recently graduated honor student from a Washington secondary school observed 2 weeks ago, "You can say you are cosmopolitan, but if you've never been confronted by a large group of people speaking a different language, you are bound to be intimidated [by the situation]. To learn to deal with them and integrate yourself with them is a skill I'm glad I acquired.... To learn these other people's world view gives you a better sense of your own." (*Washington Post,* 15 June, 1989, p. C2).

How We Value Other Peoples

Another student in the aforementioned report, commenting on his experiences in a Virginia high school, observed, "The thing I've gotten in my school is a wonderful mix of people... I played on the soccer team, [which]...was primarily Hispanic....Then...on a volleyball team with all Vietnamese guys and it is...really neat to get to know [them] and how they live their lives. And then I had the basketball team and that was mostly Black."

Because presumably normal, well adjusted persons usually remain in their home countries all their lives, except for brief visits to other lands, those who migrate are not behaving as we expect them to do. When we automatically question why they leave home, instead of remaining "where they belong," we can detect an automatic triggering of suspicion; the weight is on them to demonstrate that they have acted reasonably in opting to leave their home and country to live among strangers. There is a tendency to assume that they have no right to intrude into the territory of others unless there is a dire emergency that forces them to relocate. They are perceived as interlopers; their decision to migrate to another land is accepted grudgingly, even by others who have done the same thing in years past, or whose parents migrated to that same country in an earlier generation. The phenomenon of possessiveness toward one's adopted land, vis-à-vis strangers who have less seniority, is common. Sometimes it takes the form of assumed solidarity with the more elite classes of the adopted land and rejection of newcomers who make no pretense that they should have elite status. Such status is not always easily defined. There is great concern among some immigrant groups in the United States, for example, that they are homeowners with stable, God-fearing families, and thus superior to those who are single, not-very-secure newcomers who have not yet proved themselves. When the two groups being compared are different in nationality, color, religion, education, or economic status, for example, presumptions of inferiority and superiority can easily develop.

Few people are accurately informed about the details of the lives and cultures of others who do not share the same ethnic background; strange notions flourish when there is neither information nor interaction. The sense of social distance is likely to be even greater when the newcomers are from a country where counseling is not widely known, because they are unfamiliar with ways of using counseling to ease the painful process of closing the social distance between them and their new neighbors. For example, a Pakistani family, expelled from Idi Amin's Uganda in the 1970s, would hardly have thought of the availability of counseling as a resource in the early months of residence in Britain or the United States. Yet their children, enrolled in unfamiliar schools and taught by teachers whose accents were as strange as their expectations, sorely needed to use the opportunities for counseling. At the same time, counselors were challenged by the extreme difficulty of helping the newcomers make use of the unfamiliar services when the counselors knew so little of their customs, religion, and former life-styles.

Recent events in China have given rise to speculation that there may be a demand for asylum from Chinese students in Britain and the United States, particularly when they have lived in the West long enough to have partially adjusted to the new patterns of existence. They have yet to learn how much more complex is a permanent or semi-permanent transfer of one's life to Western society, so different from their own. The couple who took refuge in the American Embassy in Beijing sought safety, and were safe at least temporarily; but those who move into so different a society are likely to face such obstacles as having to be responsible for themselves in numerous ways, instead of being directed how to behave and what interests to cultivate, a serious burden to those accustomed to being supervised in numerous aspects of their lives.

Another kind of newcomer is the "refugee" from economic despair, seeking to share what she or he hopes is an opportunity to find economic freedom and advancement in another land. The United States sees many such immigrants from Central and South American countries where poverty and limited opportunity are the norm, and many hard-working and intelligent persons find it almost impossible to survive. Similarly, those who leave Africa or the Caribbean for an education in a highly developed country may have a difficult time making the adjustment.

These examples illustrate how inefficiently equipped we are to assess the value of our immigrants and their descendents. Perhaps we would benefit from a review of the contributions of Benjamin Disraeli and Michael Albert Einstein, Enrico Fermi, George Washington Carver, and other hyphenated Americans of like quality recognized at the United States Bicentennial ceremonies.

Helping the Newcomer

Counseling may be the crucial ingredient in the struggle of a newcomer to adjust to life in a totally different environment. Recently, the *Washington Post* published the story of a young Vietnamese who was brought by his parents to the United States at the age of 5. He was just learning to speak his own language when he was saddled with the necessity of learning English. Looking back on his introduction to school, he said:

"I was immediately separated from the other students because I couldn't speak English and they could. I...developed into a juvenile delinquent....[O]ne teacher in first grade managed to change my life...She made me see how much there was to learn. Many of my relatives...have been medical doctors, so I went into high school thinking, 'Medicine. That's for me.'"

But he had a counselor who advised him to try a variety of studies before settling on his life's work. It opened a whole world of possibilities to this lad. He discovered that he had a gift for writing and a whole variety of exciting fields to explore. He was valedictorian of his class and is now considering journalism, archaeology, and architecture as he prepares to enter Duke University. Counseling opened a whole range of opportunities to him.

Unfortunately, not all refugees are so young and adaptable. Some are unlikely to learn readily the language of their new country; many of these have come to find a better way to make a living or to accompany younger members of the family. Counseling can make a great difference in the lives of adult immigrants who find themselves responsible for their children in a vastly unfamiliar society, often with few acquaintances who understand their linguistic and cultural background. Many suffer from loneliness and a sense of being useless to relatives who are struggling to keep afloat in a sea of challenges. Help with meeting others who share a similar predicament or are otherwise lonely can comfort these less resilient persons, and even persons who do not know their culture or language can communicate empathy as they share quiet enjoyment of music or square dancing, a drive through a beautiful park, or a quiet afternoon of needlework, knitting, or other crafts. Nonverbal communication can be highly effective, and it expands the scope of otherwise monotonous lives.

There are many ways to reach people who are working hard to establish themselves in a new society. They may be very busy, because the lives of their children and older dependent relatives revolve around them, but they need to know how to use the transportation systems, what to do in the case of emergency illness, what schools require in the way of supplies, uniforms, and consultations with teachers, and a hundred other details that are familiar to those who have grown up in the host country. Simply letting them know where they can get advice on matters that puzzle them can help. Providing counseling services that can be of crucial importance is not difficult for well-trained personnel, but much of the need fails to be met when leadership is not sensitive to the needs of those who confront the industrial culture of the developed West for the first time.

The alternative to counseling services is a prolonged period of adjustment, during which frustrated newcomers sometimes fall into ineffective or even antisocial responses to the challenges of modern life. They may become hostile, or they may sink into despair. They may feel discouraged to the point of slackening their efforts to adjust to an environment that seems to have minimal space for their needs. Correcting the resulting maladjustment is likely to be far more difficult than making an effective program the first time around.

Political Aspects of Population Diversity

It is obviously impossible to forestall all conflict arising from differences between groups. These may be especially sharp when they are between the "majority," however defined, and varieties of "newcomers" or other persons perceived as not having the full status of respected citizens, even though some of them may have been in the country for a very long period of time, indeed, as is the case of Native Americans and the descendents of African slaves, and perhaps Scots or Welsh or Irish residents of parts of Britain where they compose less than a majority.

Political issues arise chiefly from a sense of threat to one's property, accustomed way of life, or political or economic freedom by the activities or even the mere existence of a group perceived as threatening some value. A large number of refugees may seem to threaten the national budget because they must be provided for until they find employment, at a cost to the taxpayer. Union workers may feel that newcomers without established power will compete for jobs without the safeguards that a union provides regarding appropriate wage levels and working conditions. The sense of threat arises from economic concerns but becomes a political issue when the government is perceived as having responsibility regarding it.

Such issues, involving threats to the rights of persons who perceive their lives as changed by the wave of newcomers, can be characterized as issues of "turf"—a sense that the country "belongs" to those already residing in it, and that the new arrivals are, therefore, asking for charity from those who already "own" the nation. Implicit in this perception is an inequality of power and "rights" between the newcomer and the already settled citizen.

The persistence of a sense of inequality, however subtly expressed, in the status of a given group inevitably leads to troublesome political issues. Sometimes these are expressed unofficially through such device as "gentlemen's agreements" not to rent to Jews, or restrictive covenants prohibiting the sale of residences to non-Whites. Both were widely used techniques in the United States 50 or more year ago, before the United States Supreme Court held such agreements unconstitutional and thus unenforceable. To complicate matters, newcomers may be unfamiliar with democratic traditions; even if they are familiar with them, they may feel powerless to demand "rights"—especially if they have come from countries where such rights were unavailable.

When newcomers have not been treated with dignity, which is usually the case with refugees, they are likely to require counseling to establish a reasonable understanding of their rights and what government agencies are set up to assist them. They will need to understand what supportive mechanisms are in place and how to use them; they also need contact with citizens' groups organized to help them get settled and find a place to live, a job, contacts with persons of similar background, and general help in getting started. When they can establish contacts with people who understand their point of view, every problem seems easier, every obstacle more manageable. It is only after these basic concerns have been dealt with that these newcomers can even understand the "turf" issues arising from the sense of threat that those who perceive them as competitors for jobs, housing, scholarships, or tax funds feel.

The counselor, then, need not deal with the new immigrant or refugee on the basis of the competition for turf. The counselor's task, in the early stages, is to guide newcomers out of the state of shock in which they arrived into a basic ability to function in order to establish themselves and seek employment. Because some will lack even the ability to speak English, the counselor will need great creative ingenuity to learn something of the cultural background of the newcomer and to help the whole family take the first steps toward getting adjusted, putting the children in school, learning what is expected of tenants in the way of care of appliances, how and where to buy food, and what assistance will be provided to the children initially entering local schools. Resettlement is a crucial time in the life of the newcomer, and the greater the understanding of the counselor regarding the former life and experiences of the family, the better and more effective the counseling will be.

Newcomers soon become permanent residents, and the task of the counselor becomes crucial in providing broader insights and facilitating finer-tuned adjustments. Counselors cannot be experts on every ethnic group, religion, or special problem. However, they hold in their hands and hearts much of the key to the successful acculturation of newcomers. If they succeed in helping their clients understand the procedures followed in employment, schools, handling of emergencies, and the variety of human relations with which they have to deal, they will have eased the paths of their counselees considerably.

This is not to say that counselors will be able to help close every gap, to enable the former residents of exotic places to fit into the life of British or North American towns and rural areas without problems. Counseling will reduce, however, the sense of social distance between newcomers and older residents and make accommodation more likely. The client is not a product of the counselor; the client is a person to be enhanced and helped to be more effective in realizing his or her goals in life through understanding more clearly what the challenges are and determining how to meet those challenges most effectively.

What about those who are not newcomers? Both Britain and the United States have already established diversity; it may be generally greater in the cities, but its fingers reach into the rural heartland. When the Boat People of Indochina came to settle in the United States, they fanned out into hundreds of communities, benefiting from an unusually well-organized plan, with sponsoring committees, initial homestays, and jobs already identified. Many who felt in possession of turf were involved in fitting the newcomers into the established pattern, and a great many made surprisingly good adjustments, despite placements in towns where there had never been a shred of Southeast Asian culture—art, religion, or even a knowledge of its geography.

The key seems to lie in the involvement of those who have to share power, living space, and daily contact. One reason why the same adjustment has not worked for African Americans is that pride of place became an essential aspect of dignity for Whites, especially in the South, which was where the majority of Black-White relations took place before World War II. The resistance of Southern Whites to considering former slaves as equals was never effectively challenged before the National Association for the Advancement of Colored People (NAACP) developed its strategy of suing in the courts for equality before the law and winning successive victories in the challenge for access to education; the right to vote, travel, and use public facilities; and, ultimately, the right to equal treatment as citizens. But without a pattern of equal respect for all citizens, private arrangements to guard the turf so that less privileged citizens still lack access remain as vestiges of old segregation and discrimination, despite the gradual weakening of many barriers.

Talent from the less privileged groups in our two societies contributes to corporate finance, national recognition, and the standard measures of achievement: the Nobel Prize, the Kennedy Center Awards, Olympic gold medals, The Pulitzer Prize, the 400 richest Americans, corporate directorships, presidential appointments, multimillion-dollar television and sports contracts, and the like. But it has been made clear that a few Jim Thorpes do not bring Native Americans into the era of genuine equality that should be our goal for all. Lee Trevino's spectacular achievements in golf have not brought the millenium to Hispanic citizens of the United States and Canada, just as the achievement of individual Pakistanis or Arabs in Britain does not yet assure that they will have the opportunity to show what they can accomplish.

The question of turf, again, is more acute when the candidate for opportunity or recognition is viewed as more distant, socially and culturally, from those considered as the traditional holders of power. In other words, those who come from Northern Europe are better able to win acceptance than those from Asia, Africa, or Latin America. Those perceived as White and Christian find access more readily available than those of other colors and religions. Wealth and relatively lighter color, other things being equal, make opportunity somewhat more accessible, with a vast fortune considerably more important than religion and race.

We are dealing with an international phenomenon: The non-Western nations of the world are stepping into the winner's circle with the European-North American industrialized nations. Although only Japan among the non-White nations is recognized as a world industrial power, the newly industrializing nations of the Pacific Rim and Latin America, the wealth of the Arab and other oil-rich nations, and even such enclaves as Brunei and Nauru, portend a change in the ethnic composition of the roster of future world powers. With the internationalization of technical education, the trend is gathering speed.

Summary

We are part of a world that is changing rapidly—partly because we would make it so—we, as intelligent, compassionate people have chosen to help those lands and peoples who without us might live in misery until, in desperation, they become a destructive force in the world. Our impulses are often good and generous, but in our puny vision we do not see all the implications of our policies and actions.

The modern world has become far more interdependent than we sometimes realize. We draw ever nearer to people—and to peoples—who were not perceived as close acquaintances a few decades ago. We have drawn closer to them, and they to us, because it is in our mutual interest that we do so.

Yet closeness brings with it a sense of conflict regarding what we expect of our new customers, business partners, neighbors—especially when they did not appear among us in such roles in the past. We find that we were gratified to do business with new friends, but are startled that their customs and life-styles and views of manners and probity interfere with our maintaining the old etiquette and comfortable ways of operating. We have a sense of being unable to turn the clock back to the kind of past when it was easier and everyone knew what the rules were and what to expect. We long for the old times until we realize that it was our need to develop a market of new buyers for our products, to obtain new sources of capital, to have workers less demanding than the highly organized ones we had, and to do business with people with deeper pockets and more modest requirements than ours. Even the immigration of so many people was a blessing, because the newcomers would accept jobs that our traditional workers would reject and would take them at lower pay.

We have learned that the children of the newcomers work harder than ours because they have less assurance that they can survive without a struggle. We begin to question their right to claim the same opportunities we have demanded for our own. Increasingly, they have become part of the "we" about which we speak. They are citizens—often excellent ones who use every opportunity to make progress in education, capital accumulation, and citizenship. They accept responsibility and take it more seriously than we have. And, they also fail, as we fail, some of us, from time to time.

No ethnic group has all the ability and the advantages. We are beginning to understand that our ethnic identification, whatever it is, is facing competition from others who do not see things quite they way we do and who wish to learn to live by our rules, but also to improve upon them when those rules do not seem moral or reasonable or fair from the point of view of their sense of what is "right." As they feel stronger and more rooted in the new country, they seek to participate. Our sense of what is fair and right comes into conflict with whom we see as being on our turf…and turf prevails over fairness. Even when the ones we now see as interlopers are right, we protest that newcomers cannot and should not change the way we do things. They do not have the right. We are not easy when turf wins out over fairness and reason, and our discomfort makes us even harder edged "when it comes to dealing with the formula for preserving our control over the turf we should rightfully share. We hate the newcomers for putting us in the position of being unjust, because we must twist our personal or national priorities to maintain our power, our primacy over them.

We have developed a whole schema of "principles" to back up our claims; thus we have to have a parallel rationale for opposing the right of our newer citizens to share in what they have helped to build. At the same time, their energy and determination make up for the lesser energies of our younger established citizens, who have not felt that their success in life depended so heavily on hard work and dedication; privilege has taken its toll of the ambition of those who already feel entitled to the best their country has to offer.

Our two countries are at the crossroads: shall they go forward, propelled in significant measure by the wave of new energy and ambition of those who aspire to build and develop a future out of their hard work, determination, and creative intelligence, working with whatever educational and other opportunities present themselves? If we welcome the new shoulders at the wheel, we can together construct a renewed and better society. If we permit ourselves to become entangled in questions of how we divide the product of our joint efforts, we divert attention from building a better society to fighting each other. We need the best of our leadership to help us keep our collective goal before us: a society that has room for us all and that is truly fair and just to all.

We must resolve to take the high road, building together for a better country, a better system of cooperation and justice—a society that welcomes the talents of all to weave a stronger, more beautiful fabric. It will take all the wisdom and strength we possess to accomplish so ambitious a task, but it can be done. Let us hope that we will not be swept away by our faith in the elite to the extent that we miss the real world and its sometimes untidily provided benefits.

A story, probably apocryphal, about a meeting of the Admissions Committee at Harvard University some years ago, illustrates the point. It is said that a member of the committee remarked that applicants for admission were now of such splendid quality that Harvard could deny admission to any applicant who scored less than 1500 (out of 1600) on the Scholastic Aptitude Test (combined score) of the College Entrance Examination Board. So high a S.A.T. score struck several members of the committee as an excellent possibility until a quiet older member remarked, "Perhaps we should be aware that if we had had that standard all along, among our alumni who would NOT have graduated from Harvard are three presidents of the United States and our hundred most generous donors."

POLITICAL ISSUES WORKSHOPS

To complete part 4, two workshop papers are presented that place political issues into the context of needed support by counselors for two distinct cultural groups. In the first paper, Professor Albert E. Roark and Jorge A. Velasco of the Boulder Valley, Colorado, Mental Health Center discuss the group counseling, guidance, and support needed for Mexican immigrants convicted of wife battering.

In the second workshop paper in part 4, Patricia Chitty, a counselor in Nikolaevsk, Alaska, discusses the problems of settlements of Russian Old Believers trying to preserve their religious beliefs and cultural values amidst the local prejudices and hostilities of non-Russians. Also addressed is the content of a special program implemented in the school attended by the children or Russian Old Believers to help them make the transition from one culture to another without giving up their old values and cultural pride.

Group Counseling, Guidance, and Support Needed for Mexican Immigrants Convicted of Wife Battering

Albert E. Roark and Jorge A. Velasco

No family is guaranteed freedom from family violence. The extent to which it occurs, and the locations where it occurs, do not seem to be correlated with education, economic status, or occupation (Stets, 1988; Zambrano, 1985). Yet, the image remains in the public eye that family violence occurs more in the home of the laborer. Stereotypes are hard to explain and harder to eliminate (Gelles, 1987, p.120; Gelles & Straus, 1988).

For example, if one were to ask the average person on the street to describe a group of immigrant Mexican men who have been convicted of battering their female partners, he or she would likely describe them as delinquent, irresponsible, cruddy, macho men who are cruel to their women and unconcerned about their children. This description, however, only applies to some of them, if any. The men in these groups are diverse, ranging from some who have beaten their wives until they almost killed them to others who were reported for a fight by observers when they were trying to prevent a suicide. Most care deeply for their children and value their opinions highly. In many ways, they are undoubtedly just like other men in batterers' groups but a large number are there for different, perhaps unfair reasons.

These unfair reasons begin at their arrest. Most can barely speak English and have little money. Consequently, the investigating officer—who normally cannot speak Spanish—relies on the wife or observers for descriptions of the incident. Therefore, the descriptions are frequently a way of retaliating against the man, often without realizing the legal implications, and are exaggerated. In Colorado, the problem is exacerbated because Colorado law is written in such a way that the investigating officer generally feels obligated to arrest someone; it is often not clear who that should be; children who need to be cared for are all over the place and the officer(s) has a problem. They are reluctant to call for advice, and often there is none available.

Therefore, they solve the problem according to their mood, biases, or best judgment. Unfairness continues after the arrest. If necessary, prisoners are provided an interpreter, but some have to spend weeks in jail before they can find anyone who will post bond for them. They have very limited social networks (Gelles, 1987) and are frequently at the mercy of their women who refuse to help.

Despite the heterogeneity of offender groups most of the members do share some traits or characteristics that contribute at least minimally to their problems and self-defeating behavior. They believe most characteristics that get them into trouble are cultural characteristics endemic to being Mexican. However, most characteristics they identify are endemic to a poverty culture of whatever ethnic origin. Other shared behavior is basically a result of ignorance in a strange land whereas other emotions and behaviors are normal human reactions to insecurity under difficult circumstances. Alcohol seems to underlie most of their problems (Gelles, 1987), and many say with insight and understanding that "I never get into trouble when I am sober." The shared characteristics and behaviors we have observed and that the members of our group have corroborated are presented below.

Machismo—Under the machismo concept, the man's role is that he is boss and not to be questioned and many have expectations in line with this role. The woman who does not honor/humor this role, expects to be treated equally, or questions his behavior challenges his manhood. The man is expected to rule his domain and provide for it; a working woman is an admission that the man is not boos or that he is not man enough to provide for his family. A woman who does not take "proper" care of the children or of him also detracts from his manhood. Consequently, both men and women are placed in difficult roles. The man must provide for his family without assistance and act like a libertine while ruling with an iron hand whether he feels like doing so or not. If he does not or cannot, he has to admit that somehow he is not really macho and carve out a new role. For those who believe they are "macho," being macho while being an immigrant in a country with many anti-macho conditions and laws may create extreme stresses and innumerable conflicts. As can be expected, many of these conflicts, especially if the man is under stress and also frustrated and intoxicated, lead to violence.

Culture—Cultural issues are very closely tied to machismo. If Mexican immigrants married a woman from Mexico, the areas of conflict would probably be reduced because women from the same culture would know what to expect from their men and more importantly they would know the role expected of them. Women raised in the United States, however, usually have different perceptions of how men should behave and are less tolerant of machismo characteristics (Zambrano, 1985). In addition, cultural differences inevitably lead to other misunderstandings that are difficult to reconcile if the machismo issue is creating tension.

Married to Americans—The Mexican men married to American women think American women are too independent and resent their belief that women are equal to men, but they understand these thoughts and feelings. Generally the men do not accept these beliefs, but consider them a result of being American and therefore understandable. But, when a woman has also come over from Mexico and is changing to think and feel like an American, the men resent it and are angered.

Pendejada—La pendejada was used by one of our group members to describe why they got into the troubles they have such as driving under the influence (DUI) and battering. La pendejada is one way of describing—perhaps as good as any—the lack of education and understanding of what the American community expects and requires. This lack of education and understanding of the world in general, not just the United States, can be called ignorance, but perhaps it is proper to regard it as naiveté. This naiveté causes difficulties and troubles that lead to frustrations, which result in emotional or angry reactions that cause interpersonal and legal hassles.

Jealousy—Both the batterers and their wives suffer from excessive jealousy. This, combined with being away from one another a good part of the day, leads to many situations that can "set up" battering. It only takes a small incident to begin the violence; the incidents often occur at dances—a favorite form of entertainment.

Language—Not really knowing English (perhaps being illiterate in any language), not knowing United States and local laws, and being destitute puts Mexican immigrants at the mercy of landlords, employers, and anyone with whom they have business. The results are difficulties and problems that become part of their daily life.

Liquor—The main problem liquor causes for Mexican immigrants is that it reduces their inclination to think before acting, and when they do stop to think it clouds their judgment. Consequently they drive when they should not and are aggressive under no-win circumstances. A majority of our group members have been or are also members of DUI groups (Gelles, 1987; Pleck, 1987; Stets, 1988).

Government help to women—welfare—Most group members resent welfare although they have benefited from it. They tend to feel it gives women too much freedom and a feeling that they do not need men. Also, they feel the law is on the side of women and that men and their situations do not count. The general feelings they have is that women are too independent and that in part it is caused by the government.

Treatment Program

When we think of these men and their situations, it is obvious that their treatment must address three different types of needs. One, behavior change needs are generally most urgent. Battering behavior, obviously, should be stopped quickly. But, this may mean that their familial interaction needs to change and their excessive drinking has to be reduced before their violent behavior can be expected to cease. Consequently, there is generally no obvious place to intervene. Two, they usually need information regarding the United States and local governmental agencies—police, legal, social welfare, and immigration services. Finally, without losing face, there is normally no one they can ask for help who understands their circumstances and feelings. So, they need someone they can talk to honestly without braggadocio or concealment. This help must be in Spanish if it is to be understood by all who need it. Consequently the treatment groups for male batterers need to be conducted in Spanish and they need to address counseling/therapy, guidance, and support.

Counseling

Counseling.therapy in groups addresses three main topics. Battering is addressed first, alcohol, if involved, next, and then violent behavior. Wife abuse, whether physical or psychological, is always the focus of behavior change efforts as long as it continues.

Violent behavior and anger control (Stets, 1988) receive a bulk of the attention in an average group. Many of the men are plagued by an extreme desire to control either themselves or others. They consider not having sufficient control a serious failure, and the frustration caused by the failure to control events, self, or others often leads to violence. Members are helped to moderate their desire for control, and assertive behavior is taught to help them achieve more control over situations without violence. Strategies to recognize anger arousal and to avert violence such as "Time Out" are stressed.

Guidance

Help is provided in understanding U.S. culture and customs. Information about differences between the United States and Mexico in areas such as what is expected between men and women, dating patterns, a husband's duties, division of household tasks, recreation, dividing time between work and family recreation, and debt problems is provided.

Support

Being with others who have the same problems allows the men to help and be helped. Seeing that others like them can and do survive offers hope, and listening to others under equally wretched conditions being sympathetic and understanding renews their faith in people.

The issue dealt with most is betrayal by their wives as they see it. When the men are not allowed to see their children, frustration and desperation may lead to ineffective actions, at best, and depression. Often, they feel that they have no one left that they are close to or whom they can trust. Under these conditions, loneliness becomes an issue, and when accompanied by destitution and homelessness, hope and rational thought vanish and some kind of support is desperately needed. Ultimately, the mutual support and understanding provided by these groups may be all some members have.

References

Gelles, R. J. (1987). *The violent home.* Newbury Park: Sage.

Gelles, R. J., & Straus, M. A. (1988). *Intimate violence.* New York: Simon & Schuster.

Pleck, E. (1987). *Domestic tyranny: The making of social policy against family violence from colonial times to the present.* New York: Oxford University Press.

Stets, J. E. (1988). *Domestic violence and control.* New York: Springer-Verlag.

Zambrano, M. M. (1985). *Mejor sola que mal acompañada.* Seattle: The Seal Press.

A Culture in Peril: Russian Old Believers

Patricia Chitty

The Old Believers (Russian) are a culture in transition in Nikolaevsk, Alaska. For the parents, this is a frightening time because old values seem to be in jeopardy. For the young people, it is a time of confusion. They are often torn between their strict religious upbringing and a desire to experience all things modern. For the local school staff, it is a time of challenge and frustration as we grapple with local non-Russian hostilities and prejudices, the desire to help preserve a culture and language, and the reality that we may not be equipped to accomplish any of this effectively.

It occurred to me that the wonderful history of the Old Believers, their cultural heritage and the current problems, may be worth sharing at a conference covering the challenges of cultural and racial diversity in counseling.

In 1968, a handful of Russian Old Believers made their way up the Alcan Highway to a roadless, remote piece of land that became their new homeland. Most of Nikolaevsk's founding fathers, mothers, and children are still here. Originally, they had come to America, via Russia, China, and Brazil. These people and their ancestors have been on the move, as a group, for over 300 years. They are members of the religion prominent in Russia before Peter the Great mandated the Russian Orthodox religion. The ancestors of today's children were persecuted by church and state alike for refusing to change their religious beliefs. Wherever they went, they took with them their beliefs, their unique colorful way of dressing, their values, their traditions, their holy books, icons, and their children.

The tales of their survival, their strength, and their faith even today read like something from an epic novel. The Old Believers came to Alaska because they believed the moral fiber of their community in Oregon was being threatened by exposure to the modern world. To them, their religion is the very fabric that binds their community and gives purpose to their lives.

The Old Believer men became commercial fishermen in the early 1970s. Today approximately 90% of the men fish. They are now prominent and dominant members if the Alaskan fishing industry. Most of the men are drift gillnetters in Cook Inlet, Bristol Bay, and Prince William Sound. They also longline for halibut and crab and fish for shrimp. They are aggressive when catching and selling their fish, clannish on the fishing grounds, and never afraid of hard work. They own their own boat shops, trade labor, and occasionally build and sell a boat to non-Russian fishermen. All this hard work has given the Old Believers ample cash, independence, and as much isolation from the outside world as they want. This same lucrative life-style, however, has brought with it problems such as the availability and accessibility of alcohol and drugs. The addictions have affected mostly the men, young and old alike, but the women also seem to be experiencing difficulties with alcohol abuse. Sometimes these problems carry over into the school, although they are nowhere near as pronounced here as they are in the larger public schools throughout the state of Alaska.

The community was thriving, economically, socially, and religiously until approximately 5 years ago. At that time, there was a severe split in the church. One group, considered the more modern and liberal, sent three of their men to study for the priesthood in Rumania and members were rebaptized according to the priesthood. The other group felt they had been 300 years without a priest and did not need one now. They also had no desire to change their fundamental religious beliefs for more modern ones. The bitterness became so violent, at one point, that the Alaska state troopers had to intervene. The current atmosphere is less tense because the more conservative families have moved to other areas closer to the head of the bay. Those who remained no longer socialize with the more modern Old Believers, and both groups now have churches of their own in the village.

The children from both factions attend the local public school, which is under the jurisdiction of the Kenai Peninsula Borough School District. The principal, Mr. Bob Moore, has been in this role for 15 years, during which time he has earned the support, respect, and trust of the community. The children, from kindergarten through grade 12, are taught that they must be tolerant of one another, and work and play together. They are also expected to speak to one another. The children actually do not seem to understand the depth of the community split and are often confused by adult behavior, speaking and writing about it frequently.

The wounds within the community are deep. None of us fully understand just how deep they really go nor do we know how long it will be before they heal, if ever. In addition to the religious changes in the village, the people are faced with other contemporary problems and the school is directly involved in these.

The Old Believers are not pursuing change from the outside world but it is coming, and the school district has been the catalyst for this concern and change. It established new attendance boundary lines last spring in order to alleviate the overcrowding conditions in a nearby city school. The Old Believers did not mind having more children come to their school. Currently about 12 non-Russian children fit in well. Everyone makes an effort to cooperate and tolerate everyone else. The non-Russian parents have been great allies to the Old Believers where preserving the culture and language are concerned.

The city parents, however, feel differently. Their innate fears, concerns, and prejudices surfaced at public hearings last spring and again this fall. The comments were published in local newspapers and the children here were really hurt. At all age levels, they kept asking, "Why don't people like us?" "Do you (teachers) still like us?"

At one point, the teachers in our school felt obliged to speak out on behalf of the children, school, and parents. The non-Russian parents and staff in the city school began referring to the Nikolaevsk school as substandard and "foreign" with a substandard staff. Parents said they didn't want their children going to school with "Russians" or "religious fanatics." Those comments were false, misleading, and, in general, outrageous to anyone who knew the school and staff, but they deeply offended the teachers here, all of whom live in this nearby city/community.

When my husband and I were offered the opportunity to transfer to Alaska this fall we thought we'd been handed a gift from the gods. Nikolaevsk is known, districtwide, for its outstanding administrator, great students, experienced and loyal staff, and parental cooperation. Upon our arrival, we discovered a staff that had been fairly devastated by criticism and the unfairness to the students.

Fortunately, a parent of one of the non-Russian students was not devastated by the happenings. She was infuriated at the district's insensitivity to the Old Believers, the fact that they had not even conferred with the local parents before holding public hearings nor before the decision to restructure the school setting and calendar. This parent subsequently organized the non-Russian parents and they later contacted leaders of the Russian parents. Together, they formed a Parent Advisory Committee consisting of both Russian and non-Russian parents. They took on the district at a public board meeting, resulting in instant action and reconsideration. The district then formed a task force to develop a plan to help alleviate the overcrowding.in the city school. The solution was not only plausible but it was so obvious throughout this process that it should have been tested prior to creating the turmoil last spring.

The Central Office administration still seems reluctant to accept the report from the task force. The reason seems to be a financial one. It would be desirable to see the district leaders concern themselves equally with cultural differences and aid in cultural preservation. It is a tense and frustrating time for staff and students alike. An attempt is being made to deal with this by ventilating these feelings. If the school does enlarge its enrollment with children who are not Old Believers, there will undoubtedly be change. An effort is being made to prepare for this in the curriculum and in the counseling program. The following steps are in progress:

1. A "Children Are People" (CAP) program in the elementary school has been initiated. The children meet weekly to discuss problems of their choice. They write their concerns anonymously on 4 x 6 index cards and place them in a container. On Friday, an hour is spent discussing these concerns and the children offer solutions. The teacher provides advice only if his or her opinion is asked or if the discussion tends to wander off track.

If the children want information on topics such as AIDS, drugs, or divorce, they merely write their request on the card. The teacher then provides that information, showing a related filmstrip that is easily obtained from the district's Media Center or a community agency. A speaker from the Homer area may also be engaged to address the topic. The Russian language teacher coordinated these discussions at the kindergarten, first, and second-grade levels. They are usually conducted in Russian, but grades 3 and 4 hold their sessions in English.

The counselor has been greatly impressed by the loving advice these children give each other. They are so caring. Sometimes it's obvious that a child will not understand exactly what is said in English, but the children translate to Russian when necessary. Free use of their native Russian is encouraged in every room at any time.

During the last 9 weeks of school, grades 3–4 take the CAP program a step further by incorporating lessons from *Feeling Good About Me* by Kenneth Morrison and Marcia Thompson.

2. The Natural Helper and Friendly Helper program is designed to facilitate interaction and relationships. The students select their peer leaders. The program instills confidence for the following reasons:

- The students themselves are keen to explore and are willing to become involved and complete the training outside of school hours;
- The program has been widely implemented throughout Alaskan schools with ongoing positive results. There are competent, qualified trainers in the area who are also available for follow-up.

- The program will provide the students with specific skills for listening, helping, and interacting with other students. They have tremendous potential in this area because they really support and care for each other. This experience will enhance the students' already healthy self-image and, perhaps, give nearby neighbors a greater respect for Russian students.

3. The Parent Advisory Committee (PAC), will assist in the quest to preserve the Russian Language Program K–12. All students, Russian and non-Russian, currently have a minimum of 1 hour per day in Russian classes. The children are dominant in their native language. They are so proficient in reading, writing, and speaking Russian that they often serve as translators and interpreters for visiting Russians of all ages. Students operate the Nikolaevsk Publishing Company, which is known nationwide. This company has been a source of great local pride.

4. An endeavor is being made to expand the high school curriculum to meet the needs of students who have begun preparing for college and technical schools. This is a new transition for parents and students alike and began about 4 years ago. One or two students per year have been going to college elsewhere. The girls are also beginning to attent college. Previously, they married early, between the ages 15 and 18, and often did not finish high school. Current needs center around advanced mathematics and science classes required by most colleges.

5. Staff and students may participate in conflict resolution training for staff and students. The Juneau School District began this program 3 years ago. This expertise will prepare the district to confront competently and positively possible problems resulting from additional enrollment.

Although current sensitivity to the Old Believers culture does not sit well with some nearby non-Russian neighbors and the community seems to experience continued difficulty breaking down stereotyped opinions of Russians, the efforts are necessary and helpful in preserving the essentials of their culture in a changing world.

Recommendations for Action

Edwin L. Herr and John A. McFadden

In addition to the plenary papers and workshop presentations included in the previous sections of this monograph, the Brunel Conference also provided for discussion groups to interact each day about the content and the processes they were experiencing. As part of that activity, they were asked to formulate recommendations for action in five areas related to the challenges of cultural diversity for counseling. These areas include: public policy, counseling theory, counseling research, counselor training and counselor practice. The recommendations in each of these areas follow:

Public Policy

- Policymakers need to consult routinely with representatives of culturally different groups when designing policies that will affect them.
- The terms *majority* and *minority* are out of date. Seven-eighths of the world is now non-Anglo. Thus, transformations are needed in the thinking and the language about the different groups at issue. More attention needs to be given in public policy to racial and cultural differences and how the needs of persons in these groups differ in housing, education, health care, and other concerns.
- Reductions in funding for schools in the United States and the United Kingdom are continuing at a time when multiculturalism and diversity must be systematically dealt with in a developmental way through the school experience. Thus, funding for schooling and for new models of multiculturalism in schools needs to be advanced.
- Professional organizations need to educate policymakers as well as potential users of counseling more fully about what counseling is and the needs for more counselors, particularly those from culturally different backgrounds.
- Professional organizations need to put pressure on accrediting organizations (as policy-making bodies) to keep multiculturalism on the agenda, and in turn for accrediting associations to keep the pressure on educational and other social institutions to see multiculturalism as integral to the organization's vitality, not a fragmented or compartmentalized matter.

- Policymakers need to be encouraged to provide appropriate allocations of funding to do appropriate research by people of color on issues in mental health delivery and other areas. Currently it is difficult to separate myth from fact about the needs for and ways to serve people of color effectively.
- Public policymakers have to be encouraged to see problems whole. For example, in the past, deinstitutionalization of mental patients in the United States and the United Kingdom has proceeded without an effective infrastructure in communities to provide support and services to these people or to find ways to reduce social stress and to diminish the roots of violence.
- Public policy, similarly, must look at the problems of immigrants in wholistic and systematic ways to provide multidimensional mechanisms for integrating these persons into society.
- Public policymakers must be helped to understand that benevolence as a public policy is a failure because (a) the government may not *know* what a minority really wants; and (b) the dependence upon the government created is dehumanizing and prolongs the stifling of cultural aspiration/integration.
- Public policy must support mental health delivery systems that are color/culture blind but that use cultural references as criteria for designing programs that are likely to be effective.
- Public policy needs to make counseling and social services and family services more accessible, more coordinated, and more multidimensional if they are to be culturally sensitive.
- Public policy needs to promote the integration of indigenous systems of counseling and helping in each culture into the more formal system that tends to evolve through legislation and other policies.
- The British Association for Counselling and the American Association for Counseling and Development must continue to see their roles as campaigning for or serving as advocates for basic human rights—freedom, access to education, equal protection under the law—health care, and employment. We must guard against policies in government that systematically do harm to any of the racial or ethnic groups existing in pluralistic societies. We must be alert against any policies that institutionalize racism or bigotry.
- AACD and BAC must continue and intensify their efforts to reduce the fear of their members and of policymakers of a multicultural/multiracial world. More conferences like this one are useful in that regard.

Counseling Theory

- Develop a theory that is based on empowerment and change.
- Emphasize a theoretical orientation to a "no loss" paradigm rather that a "win/lose" model.
- Address through counseling theory the premise that societies differ and social systems differ.
- Avoid confinement solely to traditional academic approaches; be as eclectic as possible, applying theories to clients and not clients to theories.
- Explore the adoption of a format to include education, application, and goal attainment.

Counseling Research

- Engage in collecting more oral histories of cultures, and produce media materials in the pursuit of new paradigms.
- Conduct research that has viable potential for translation into public policy and implications for training.
- Formulate multicultural training standards and ethical practice standards with research as a basis for safeguards in practice.
- Spearhead research on terminology for culturally related counseling focus.
- Engage in research on how various cultures understand what it means to dream and have vision.
- Support research with an emphasis on individual and personal histories.

Counselor Training

- Assist counselor trainees to develop skills in conducting staff development programs so that others (e.g., teachers) may acquire an improved level of multicultural awareness.
- Ensure that programs provide opportunities for students in counselor training to look at their own prejudices and biases.
- Encourage students to focus on their self-esteem and worth.
- Set standards for initial understanding and continual updating of basic ethnicity and multiculturality for counselors.

Counselor Practice

- Cultural differences may initially be partially overcome through client-centered "Rogerian" attitudes, *but* the practitioner must be culturally attuned (e.g., aware of clients' cosmology and worldview). Cross-cultural strategy found effective in counseling must be disseminated and incorporated in practice. A major need is to develop more culturally specific psychometric instrumentation.
- The goal of counseling is change—that's universal; the ways to bring about change are not universal, they are culturally dependent.
- Counselors must look at the self first—their awareness of self is crucial in helping others. Within this context counselors must know their own cultural background and baggage, be trained in their own culture first, then in other cultures.
- Although it may be possible to create a transactional paradigm, it would not likely have answers, but guidelines.
- Counselors cannot do it all in meeting the needs of culturally different populations. Teachers must help as well, but they must be trained.
- Counseling must be viewed as an empowerment process, both at an individual and a group level. Part of the empowerment process around which the counselor role should be oriented needs to help individuals develop an internal rather than an external locus of control. Certainly, if counselors have as goals change and empowerment, they must also see themselves as advocates for multicultural concerns and as activists in bringing to the attention of policymakers and others

barriers to the economic and social development of persons who are culturally and racially different.

- A major recommendation is the need to increase the numbers of minority counselors in the United Kingdom and the United Stated to provide more access for persons of color or cultural difference to express themselves in the native language as necessary and to have the opportunity to escalate the development of trust with counselors who share their backgrounds. The counseling profession needs to be seen as more representative of the broader community and of persons of color.
- Counselors need to lead the emphases of institutions in making "soup"—sharing cross-cultural integration by helping all social groups to provide input into international/transactional knowledge bases, to create an ambience of integrating cultures so as to decrease the sense of turf ownership.
- Counselors must employ multiple strategies to help people in dealing with the illnesses of society. Among them are conflict resolution, stress reduction, and problem solving.
- The labeling of clients/students in cultural or other terms must be done with utmost care and consideration. The criteria for diagnosing/labeling must be clearly understood. An important need is coalitions of racially and culturally different counselors on diagnosis, assessment, and treatment teams. It is also necessary for counselors to understand more fully the ideology of large value or religious systems—such as that of Islam. In doing so, the likelihood that counselors will use deficit models to explain the behavior of persons whose traditions and beliefs are different will be lessened.
- It is necessary in practice to acknowledge more fully the political aspects and implications of counseling.

Biographies

Biographies of Plenary Speakers and Leaders of the American Association for Counseling and Development and the British Association for Counselling

Paul Boateng, QC, has represented his East London (Walthamstow) and Brent South constituencies in Parliament since 1981. Boateng earned his law degree from Bristol University's College of Law, becoming a solicitor in 1975. He has been extremely active in the cause of human rights and has been a vigorous advocate of improved race relations, inner-city housing, and overseas development. Boateng has effectively utilized churches, community agencies, schools, and private philanthropies to forward the access of ethnic minorities to economic and social opportunity.

Omar Daniels, MD, is senior consulting psychiatrist with Princess Alexandra Hospital in Harlow, Essex. His special interests are alcoholism and other substance abuse, and he chairs a community-based organization that offers counselling for these problems. Dr. Daniels is also involved in marriage and family therapy and is particularly concerned with the influence of cultural factors over psychiatric diagnoses. Beyond his hospital association, he is a visiting tutor for the Tavistock Clinic.

Edwin L. Herr, EdD, is distinguished professor and head, Department of Counselor Education, Counseling Psychology and Rehabilitation Services Education, The Pennsylvania State University. Dr. Herr is internationally known for his work in career development and is the author of 28 books and monographs and more than 275 journal articles. A former President of AACD and two of its divisions, Dr. Herr is an active contributor to several international counseling groups and has most recently published *Counseling in a Dynamic Society: Opportunities and Challenges* (AACD, 1989).

Colin Lago, MEd, serves as a counsellor at the University of Sheffield and is an accredited practitioner member of the Association for Student Counselling. Lago has held leadership positions across several professional societies and is active in staff development and the production of original materials, including videotapes. His particular interests include working with university staff on stress management.

Courtland E. Lee, PhD, is associate professor and head of counselor education at the University of Virginia. Dr. Lee also serves as president of the Association of Multicultural Counseling and Development, and as editor of its distinguished journal. He has published numerous articles on adolescent career development and counseling ethnic minorities and presently chairs AACD's Council of Journal Editors. Dr. Lee's current interests are the application of counseling theories and models to inner-city school systems where longitudinal research can be conducted with the support of all faculty, parents, and relevant community agencies.

John A. McFadden, PhD, is the Benjamin E. Mays Distinguished Professor in the University of South Carolina's Department of Educational Psychology. Dr. McFadden has been especially active in the field of multicultural counseling and has held leadership positions in AACD that have relied on his comprehension of ethnic minority needs and aspirations. As incoming chairperson of AACD's Media Committee, Dr. McFadden will be responsible for guiding the association's publishing decisions in terms of books, videos, films, and tapes concerned with counseling and human development. He continues to hold significant and voluntary public service positions and most recently served as Senior Vice President for Intercultural Affairs and Professional Development at USC.

Sara E. Melendez, EdD, is the vice provost of the University of Bridgeport in Bridgeport, Connecticut. Prior to this recent appointment, Dr. Melendez served as associate director, Office of Minority Concerns, with the American Council on Education in Washington, DC. She has published widely and has directed master's degree programs in bilingual education, English and Spanish, and an ESL-math program for adults. Dr. Melendez is deeply concerned with the often overlooked problems of those persons whose native language is not English and is a strong advocate of cross-cultural communication skills that do not limit themselves to one spoken language.

Mabel M. Smythe-Haith, PhD, professor emerita, Northwestern University (Illinois), and former ambassador to New Guinea and Cameroon is an internationally known writer on economic and educational issues, African refugees, and minority and women's affairs. Dr. Smythe-Haith has traveled and published extensively and has served her country with distinction as a U.S. Department of State representative and delegate. She continues to be active on several boards concerned with equity issues and is the recipient of many awards as an advocate of displaced and underutilized persons in all world societies.

Joyce Thompson is a registered mental nurse (RMN) and community psychiatric nurse (CPN) and also holds a diploma in counseling skills. She presently serves as a management consultant and counseling skills trainer along with her duties as a senior nurse education manager in a major London teaching hospital. Thompson is a BAC-recognized supervisor, a member of the British Association of Black Counsellors, and an active member of the Standing Conference for the Advancement of Trainers and Supervisors (SCATS).

Association Officials

Judith Baron, MSS, is the chair of the British Association for Counselling and has worked as a social worker for more than 20 years. She currently serves as regional manager and staff training officer for a company that builds and manages sheltered housing for the frail elderly. Mrs. Baron has also published extensively on pregnancy counselling, helping the infertile and those with epilepsy, and has focused on conducting applied research in the National Health Service.

Elisabeth Davies is General Manager, British Association for Counselling, and coordinates all business operations for BAC officers and members in the United Kingdom and overseas. Mrs. Davies took her degree in history from Cambridge University and has had an extensive career as a teacher and administrator in local government. Her interest in counselling evolved during her experience as a volunteer "service worker" and has been enriched by residence in Italy, Singapore, and San Francisco.

Sunny Hansen, PhD, is president-elect, 1988–1989, of the American Association for Counseling and Development, and assumes office on July 1, 1989. Dr. Hansen is professor of counseling at the University of Minnesota and is internationally know in the fields of career development and gender-fair counseling. Active in both the International Round Table for the Advancement of Counselling and the International Association for Educational and Vocational Guidance, as are many AACD and BAC members, she is adopting an aggressive "international community" focus for her year in office. Dr. Hansen is the author of more than 6 books and over 100 journal articles and monographs.

Douglas Hooper, PhD, is honorary president of the British Association for Counselling and currently serves as visiting professor at Bristol University. Dr. Hooper's training is in clinical and social psychology, and his experience in counselling and psychotherapy spans time and nations (the U.S., Australia, and his own England). His present research is concerned with the role of the courts in resolving family problems, and he continues in mental health consultation and practice.

Derek Hope, PhD, is senior counsellor at Brunel and is the university's Advisor to Overseas Students. Dr. Hope is deputy chair of the British Association for Counselling and also serves as a member of Welbeck Associates, a team of professionals offering counselling, consultancy, and training services to organizations and industry. As secretary of the International Round Table for the Advancement of Counselling (IRTAC) for the past 14 years, he has worldwide counselling contacts with individuals and kindred associations. Dr. Hope's research interests are in counsellor stress and burnout as factors of counsellor effectiveness.

Patrick J. McDonough, EdD, was the executive director of the American Association for Counseling and Development until 1990. Dr. McDonough served in this capacity since 1983 and devoted himself to the association for more than 22 years in other critical capacities. He supervised over 80 employees at the headquarters offices in Alexandria, Virginia, executing the will of the elected Governing Council and the 56,000 members of AACD. Having received all his graduate degrees from Loyola University of Chicago, Dr. McDonough is particularly concerned with intra-association and human resource management issues.

Robert J. Nejedlo, PhD, is president, 1988–1989, of the American Association for Counseling and Development and professor of counseling at the Northern Illinois University in DeKalb. Dr. Nejedlo will have established many precedents during his tenure, including the support of this, the association's first offshore conference. While in office, he has worked diligently to bring the profession to that point where its practitioners are ready to meet the challenges of the nineties.